PAPER
BEAD
jewelry

STACKPOLE BOOKS

First Published in the United States in 2018 by Stackpole Books
An imprint of The Rowman & Littlefield Publishing Group, Inc.
4501 Forbes Blvd., Ste. 200
Lanham, MD 20706

Distributed by NATIONAL BOOK NETWORK
800-462-6420

PAPER BEADS ACCESSORY (NV80479)

Keiko Sakamoto worked as a floral designer for over 10 years before launching her jewelry business. In 1999, she opened her shop called Beads Cafe. Her vision was to create a place where people could learn jewelry making in a relaxed setting similar to a cafe. Sakamoto's work has been featured on television and in magazines. Visit her website at www.beadscafe.net

British Library Cataloguing in Publication Information available
Library of Congress Cataloging-in-Publication Data

Names: Sakamoto, Keiko, 1967- author.
Title: Paper bead jewelry : step-by-step instructions for 40+ designs / Keiko Sakamoto.
Description: Guilford, Connecticut : Stackpole Books, 2018.
Identifiers: LCCN 2018001890| ISBN 9780811719841 (hardcover/paperback) | ISBN 9780811765763 (e-book)
Subjects: LCSH: Beadwork. | Paper beads. | Jewelry making.
Classification: LCC TT860 .S334 2018 | DDC 745.594/2--dc23
LC record available at https://lccn.loc.gov/2018001890

ISBN 978-0-8117-1984-1 (hardcover/paperback)
ISBN 978-0-8117-6576-3 (e-book)

™ The paper used in this publication meets the minimum requirements of American National Standard for Information Sciences—Permanence of Paper for Printed Library Materials, ANSI/NISO Z39.48-1992.

Printed in Canada

PAPER BEAD

jewelry

Step-by-step Instructions
for *40+* Designs

KEIKO SAKAMOTO

STACKPOLE
BOOKS

Guilford, Connecticut

Introduction

Paper beads are made by rolling thin strips of paper to create fun, unique shapes. You can use just about any type of paper, from newspaper and gift wrap to basic copy paper. You can even use personal mementos, such as ticket stubs and maps, to create sentimental pieces of jewelry commemorating special trips and events.

The best thing about making paper beads is that you don't always know what the finished design will look like beforehand. Watching a thin strip of paper transform into a beautiful, three-dimensional beads is a magical process: The bead's finished shape and pattern are revealed as each layer of paper is rolled into place.

Paper beads are very lightweight, allowing you to create bold, intricate jewelry designs without fear that the finished piece will be too heavy to wear. Once rolled, the beads are sealed with a water-resistant coating, making them durable enough to wear every day.

In this book, I've combined handmade paper beads with wire, leather cord, natural gemstones, and metal components to create a collection of stylish accessories. I guarantee that your friends and family will never guess your jewelry is made out of paper!

— Keiko Sakamoto

Contents

Ombré Bracelets

Combine colored drawing paper and patterned wrapping paper in similar shades to create a beaded bracelet with an ombré effect. Use coordinating embroidery floss to add a matching ombré tassel.

Instructions on page 58

Two-Tone Bracelets

A

B

These bold bracelets will add a pop of color to any outfit. Use drawing paper to create matte beads inspired by natural stone. White works well as an accent color, but the possibilities are endless.

Instructions on page 61

Lemonade Necklace

This cheerful necklace will brighten up any
outfit. Look for a yellow and white print paper
to create beads with a marbled texture.
The addition of solid gray and white beads
produces a subtle color block effect.

Instructions on page 63

Pastel Confetti Necklace & Bracelets

These candy colored beads look sweet enough to eat! Simple white beads provide the perfect contrast to brightly-hued paper beads in this festive necklace and bracelet set.

Instructions on page 66

Floret Necklace

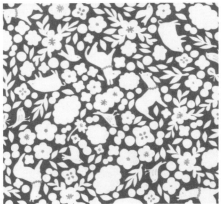

This double-strand necklace is made from two different shapes of floral-print paper beads, as well as natural stone, metal, and Czech glass beads. This unique combination creates a vibrant, sophisticated design.

Instructions on page 70

s entstand eine lange Pause. Dann
pos, wollten Sie mir nicht auch die
onen bringen, die Ihr Fräulein
ldig ist? Der Verfallstag ist erst im
ausend Kronen waren ja auch noch

Fäuste in die Rocktaschen. Er ging
Dupic folgte ihm mit vielen kleinen

ause. Er wußte, es wäre b... jetzt

Dr. med. Peter Dupic, Sprechstunden 8–9, 2–6: das
kleine Schild am Tor des Hauses Nr. 3 auf dem Markt-
platz erregte in Boran großes Aufsehen. Man sah Dupic mit einem großen, breitschultrigen, etwa dreißig-
jährigen Mann spazierengehen. Mehrere Leute er-

155

The reproductions in this book have been
the most modern electronic scanning methods
next transparencies of Beatrix Potter's origina
They enable Beatrix Potter's skill as an artist t
as never before, not even during her own

254   NOT

— Assez sauvagem... dent
son rire de belles dent
Cette réflexion fut
leur fit voir le côté
mordre sur sa beauté
— Mais cela est vra
de courir ainsi par les
— Voilà une jupe
fontaine.
— Ma chère, poursu
vous ferez ramasser pa
ceinture dorée.
— Petite, petite, rep
cable, si tu mettais ho
serait moins brûlé par le
C'était vraiment un
intelligent que Phœbus
leurs langues envenimé
se tordaient autour de la
et gracieuses. Elles foui
la parole dans sa pauvr
peaux. C'étaient des rire
Les sarcasmes pleuvaie
hautaine, et les regards
dames romaines qui s'a
dans le sein d'une belle
chasseresses tournant, le
autour d'une pauvre bi
leur interdit de dévorer.
Qu'était-ce, après tou
qu'une misérable danseu
tenir aucun compte de s
elle, à elle-même, à haute
malpropre, d'assez abjec
La bohémienne n'était
De temps en temps une
enflammait ses yeux ou
semblait hésiter sur ses
petite grimace que le le
Immobile, elle attachait
et doux. Il y avait aussi
regard. On eût dit qu'elle
Phœbus, lui, riait, et p
un mélange d'impertinenc
— Laissez-les dire, pe

On trouvera ci-dessous et dans les pages qui suivent un recueil des plus
remarquables lettres de Mozart. Traduction de I. Kaschler.

✱ Le ton badin du jeune Wolfgang

*(La veille de ses quatorze ans, Wolfgang, qui se trouve à Milan, écrit à sa
sœur restée au pays.)*
Milan, 26 janvier 1770. – Je me réjouis de tout mon cœur que te sois
si bien amusée dans la partie de traîneau que me décris, et je te souhai-
terais mille occasions d'amusement, qui ...ent passer ta vi...
Mais une chose m'afflige, c'est que tu ai... souffrir et soup... a...
ce pauvre M. de Mœlk, que tu ne sois ...entée en traîneau avec ...,
pour lui donner moyen de verser avec ...mbien n'aura-t-i...
de mouchoirs ce jour-là, pour sécher les la... que tu lui auras fa...
Il est probable qu'il se sera d'avance in...rois onces de ta... p...r
se purifier. Je ne sais rien de nouveau, si c... que M. Gellert, le p... de
Leipzig, est mort, et qu'après sa mort il n... fait de poésie. ...nt
de commencer cette lettre, j'ai terminé un ... de *Demetrio* ...mence
ainsi:

Misero tu non sei;
Tu spieghi il tuo dolore.
E se non desti amore,
Ritrovi almen pietà.

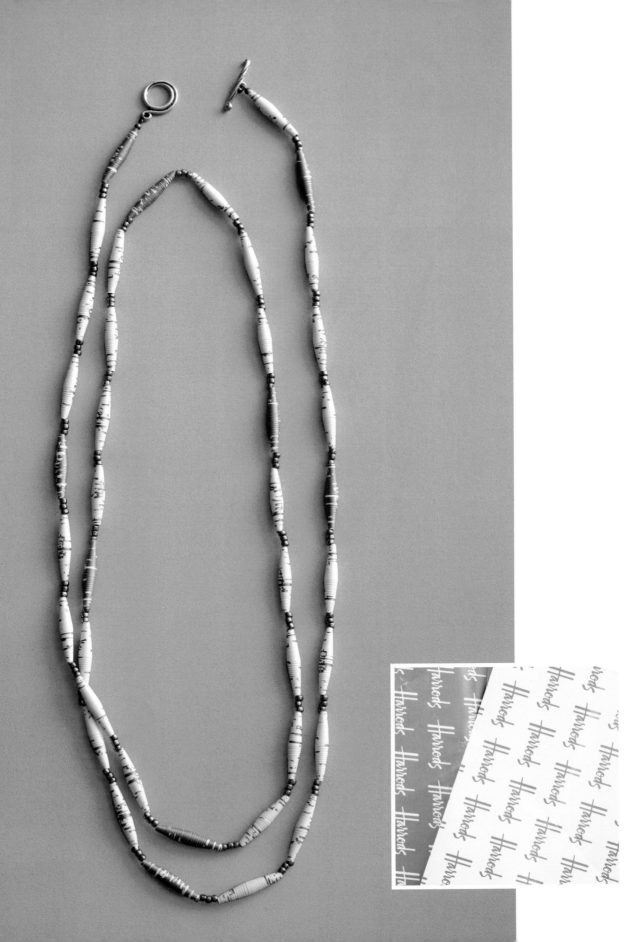

Golden Deco Necklace

Sometimes the most unexpected materials can make the most elegant beads—this sophisticated necklace is made from department store wrapping paper! Featuring long, tubular beads, this necklace works up quickly. Plus, it can be styled many different ways, making it extremely versatile.

Instructions on page 72

15

Paper Pearl Necklace

These beautiful "pearls" are made by rolling newspaper into beads, then coating with white acrylic paint. The finished beads have a similar feel and weight to cotton pearls. This classic necklace can be worn as a double strand, a single knotted strand, or a collar as shown at the right.

Instructions on page 45

La mère, Anna Maria
M... bonne ménagère,
mère attentive et affec-
tu... soumise à l'auto-
rité ... son mari.

Rose Gold & Pink Pendant & Earrings

This sweet pendant is constructed with striped washi tape, gold wire, and rose pink beads. Try changing the bead color and washi tape pattern for a completely different look.

Instructions on page 51

Braided Flowers Bracelet & Ring

Lustrous Czech glass beads are woven with gray and pink paper beads to create this feminine bracelet and ring set inspired by flowers.

Instructions on page 75

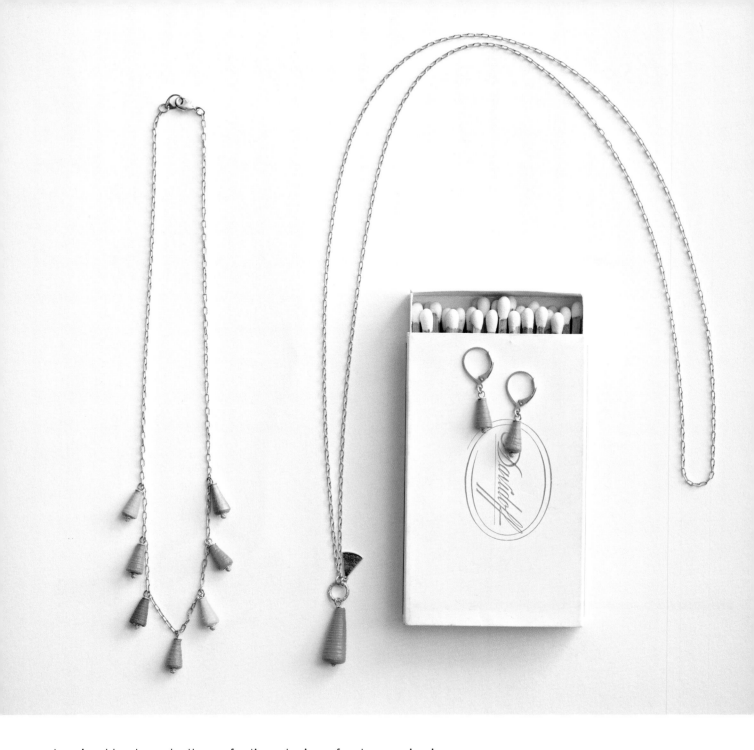

Inspired by tassels, these festive designs feature swinging, cone-shaped beads rolled from newspaper, then covered in vibrant shades of acrylic paint and finished with grommets. The necklaces look great layered, but can also be worn independently—they'll transform a boring t-shirt and jeans into the perfect party outfit!

Instructions on page 78

Tassel Necklace, Pendant & Earrings

Aquamarine Necklace & Earrings

This stunning statement necklace offers contemporary design in a cool mint, white, and gunmetal color scheme. Make the coordinating earrings for a matching set.

Instructions on page 82

23

Nautical Necklace & Bracelet

Featuring knotted rope, nautical charms, and striped beads, this maritime-inspired necklace and bracelet set makes a great addition to any summer wardrobe. Learn how to make striped paper beads in the special technique guide on page 48.

Instructions on page 48

Glam Garnet Necklace

At first glance, this glamorous multistrand necklace appears as if it's made from natural stone, not paper. With a jewel tone color scheme and sophisticated gold findings, this elegant necklace is perfect for special occasions.

Instructions on page 86

Festive Friendship Bracelets

Inspired by Japanese misanga good luck bracelets, these three designs combine colorful paper beads and knotted cords. Layer a few bracelets for a Bohemian look.

Instructions on pages 90-97

Boho Wrap Bracelets

Use the ladderwork technique to string a row of paper beads between two leather cords and create a stylish wrap bracelet. This design incorporates both text and floral print paper for a modern look.

Instructions on page 98

The Paper Memento Collection

Celebrations of special occasions are often marked by paper: from party invitations and ticket stubs to wrapping paper and stamps. Why not save these meaningful pieces of paper and use them to create one-of-a-kind accessories with sentimental value?

Bangle Bracelet

Commemorate your travels with a beaded bangle bracelet souvenir. Recycle a map of Paris to create uniquely-shaped conical beads, then transform the metallic wrapping paper from a box of sponge cake into the lustrous gold bead at the center of the bracelet.

Instructions on page 101

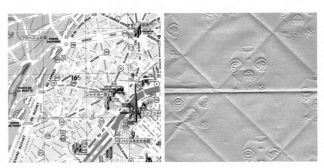

Paper: Paris map/Bunmeido's Kasutera sponge cake wrapping paper

30

Chain Petite Necklace &
Ribbon Bracelets

Brightly patterned paper can be "fussy cut" to create unique beads with bold prints. Roll the beads into an hourglass shape for the necklace design, or string onto elastic ribbon for a fun bracelet.

Instructions on page 103

Paper: Demel Kohlmarkt
bakery paper from Austria

Leather Cord Bracelet

Save the wine label from a special evening, such as a wedding or anniversary dinner, then transform it into a beautiful bracelet to commemorate the event.

Instructions on page 55

Paper: Domaine Houchart wine label

Silk Ribbon Bracelet

With their bright and cheerful designs, candy wrappers make excellent paper beads. This bracelet was crafted with cylindrical beads covered in French caramel wrappers, then strung onto a watercolor silk ribbon. With their folk-inspired print and simple shape, these beads are reminiscent of hand-painted wooden beads.

Instructions on page 108

Paper: Bonbons Barnier Sucette Bretagne lollipop wrapper

Postage Stamp Bracelets

These simple bracelets showcase the artful design of vintage stamps. Add decorative metal beads and string onto luxurious velvet ribbon for a quick bracelet with antique charm.

Instructions on page 110

Paper: Vintage stamps

Long Pendant Necklace & Brooch

Constructed from a playbill, this necklace and brooch set makes the perfect gift for an actress or theater-loving friend. Brass findings lend an air of casual style to this eclectic set.

Instructions on page 112

Paper: Theater program

33

The Textile Collection

In addition to paper, you can use the same bead making techniques to create handmade beads from fabric, leather, ribbon, and other textiles. Incorporate interesting materials and textures into your jewelry designs for added style.

Liberty & Ribbon Long Necklace

Use Liberty of London print bias tape and grosgrain ribbon to create cylindrical beads full of texture and pattern. Flower-shaped metal bead spacers conceal the bead holes and create a professional-looking finish, making this necklace worthy of a spot in a trendy boutique.

Instructions on page 116

Colorful Suede Bracelet

Cut strips of brightly colored suede into thin isosceles triangles, then roll to make these cute and playful beads. The soft texture of this bracelet is perfect for your autumn and winter wardrobe.

Instructions on page 119

Suede Tassel Pendant

Create this uniquely curved bead by rolling a rectangular strip of suede, then stringing it onto a pin and bending it into shape. This bohemian style pendant pairs well with boxy sweaters and t-shirts.

Instructions on page 121

The Earring Collection

Tropical Hoops

Elegant Dangles

Fiesta Dangles

Pearl Hoops

Ocean Drops

Moon Drops

Modern Hoops

All of these elegant earring designs are quick and easy to make. In fact, they serve as wonderful gifts. As an added bonus, paper beads are lightweight and very comfortable to wear.

Instructions on page 124

MATERIALS, TECHNIQUES & INSTRUCTIONS

Paper

You can use almost any paper for bead making, as long as it's not too thick or hard to roll. In fact, the most unexpected paper often makes the most beautiful beads, so feel free to experiment! The following guide lists some of my favorite papers for bead making.

Colored paper: Use this paper for bold, colorful beads. Look for colored drawing or copy paper rather than construction paper, which can be very thick.

Wrapping paper and scrapbook paper: Available in many different colors and patterns, these decorative papers make unique beads. Look for papers with small-scale prints, which are better suited for beads.

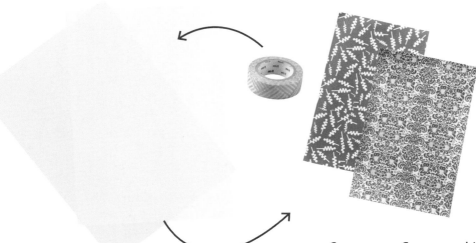

Copy paper: Common white printer paper is a very versatile material for bead making. Print your favorite patterns to create custom paper, or adhere washi tape (see page 51).

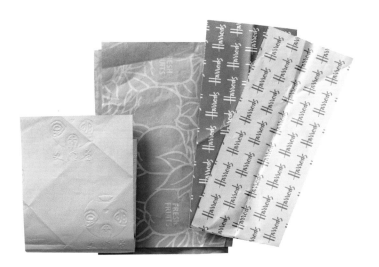

Recycled packaging: Believe it or not, your recycling bin is an excellent source for bead making materials! Food wrappers, shopping bags, and tissue paper can all be used for bead making. Don't worry about creases or wrinkles—they'll disappear once the paper is rolled into a bead.

Newspaper: This lightweight paper is perfect for rolling into beads. You can use the print as a design element, or paint the paper after it's been rolled into a bead (see page 45).

Magazines: Colorful pages from old magazines make interesting, one-of-a-kind beads.

Tickets and stamps: Even small pieces of paper like tickets and stamps can be used as stylish accents. Connect them with larger pieces as shown on page 55 or use them to cover the outside of beads made from other papers.

Tools

Paper bead making doesn't require specialized tools. If you own basic craft and jewelry making tools, you may already have everything you'll need.

Cutting mat: Protect your work surface with a mat when cutting paper.

Ruler: You'll need a ruler to measure the paper before cutting into strips. Look for a ruler that's at least 12 in (30 cm) long. A clear plastic ruler is also useful because it allows you to see the paper underneath.

Coating agent: Coat the rolled beads with an acrylic sealer, waterproof varnish, or clear nail polish to transform the paper into a stiff, sturdy bead. There are a wide variety of coating agents available on the market today—see the sidebar on page 41 for more information.

Bamboo skewers, toothpicks, and pencils: Use to roll the paper strips into beads. Choose the appropriate thickness for your desired bead diameter (see page 44). You can also use chopsticks, pens, and pencils to create beads with larger holes.

Chopstick: Sharpen the tip just like a pencil, then use the chopstick to hold the bead while you apply the coating agent or paint.

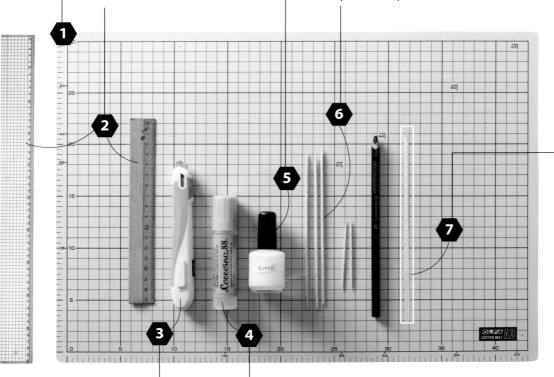

Paper knife: Dedicate a craft or utility knife for cutting paper only.

Glue: Use a high quality glue to secure the paper ends of the rolled beads.

About Coating Agents

Use an acrylic sealer, such as Mod Podge, waterproof varnish, or clear nail polish to coat your rolled beads. Acrylic sealers and varnishes are available in a wide variety of finishes, so you can choose whether you want your beads to have a matte or glossy look.

I like to transfer my coating agent to an empty nail polish bottle (as shown in the photo on page 40), so I can use the brush for neat and convenient application.

Other Tools

You'll need some basic jewelry making tools to transform your beads into beautiful jewelry and accessories.

1

2

3

4

Round nose pliers: Use the round tips to curl wires and pins.

Flat nose pliers: Use to hold findings and open jump rings.

Nipper pliers: Use to cut wire.

Beading needles: Use to string beads onto thread, especially for ladderwork.

How to Make Paper Beads

There are three basic steps for making beads: Cut the paper, roll the paper, and apply the coating agent. The following guide illustrates how to make a paper bead from start to finish.

1. Cut the paper.

2. Roll the paper.

3. Apply the coating agent.

a. Mark the cutting lines.

a. Tightly wrap the paper strip around a bamboo skewer. If your paper strip is shaped like a triangle or trapezoid, always start rolling from the wider end.

a. Insert the bead onto the sharpened tip of a chopstick (if you continue using your bamboo skewer, the bead will be hard to remove after you apply the coating agent). Use a brush to evenly apply the coating agent to the surface of the bead.

b. Align the ruler with the marks, then cut.

b. Apply a small dab of glue to the end. Use your finger to press firmly and secure the end to the bead.

Apply two coats

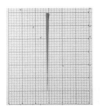

c. This paper strip has been cut into an isosceles triangle.

c. Allow the glue to dry, then twist to remove the skewer from the bead.

b. Allow the first coat to dry, then apply a second coat to ensure that the entire bead has been covered. Once the second coat dries, you're done!

How to Make Different Bead Shapes

You can make a variety of different bead shapes depending on how you cut your paper strips. The designs in this book use six basic shapes.

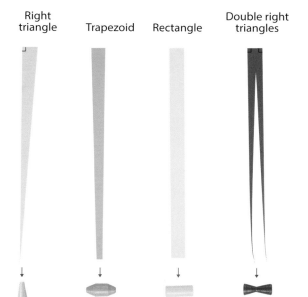

Isosceles triangle   Right triangle   Trapezoid   Rectangle   Double right triangles   Double trapezoids

There are a few things to keep in mind when rolling different bead shapes.

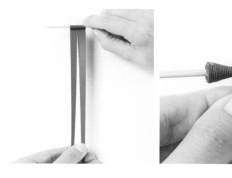

Isosceles triangle: Keep the paper strip centered when rolling to ensure that both sides of the bead are equal in width.

Double right triangles/double trapezoids: Roll the triangles or trapezoids individually. For double right triangles, make sure to align the bottom edges of the paper strip and bead, as shown for the single right triangle below.

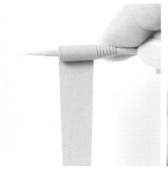

Right triangle: Keep the bottom edge of the paper strip aligned with the bottom of the bead as you roll. Use your finger or the tabletop to press the bottom of the bead and adjust the shape if necessary.

A Note About Bead Size & Shape

Your finished bead size and shape will vary based on the rolling tool you use. Even if you use equally-sized strips cut from the same paper, the finished shape of the beads and the size of the holes will vary if you use different rolling tools.

Likewise, if you use multiple types of paper with different thicknesses, the finished shape and size of the beads may vary, even if you use the same size strips and the same rolling tool.

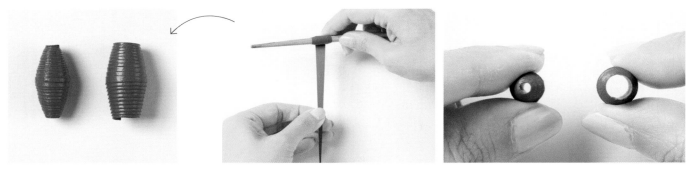

The bead on the left was rolled using a bamboo skewer, while the bead on the right was rolled using a chopstick.

Note that the size of the hole also changes. The bead on the right, which was rolled using a chopstick, works well for thick stringing materials, such as rope.

Each project includes a bead size you should aim to replicate and recommends which paper type and rolling tool to use in order to achieve this size. If you decide to experiment with different tools and materials, the following tips may be helpful:

Rolling Tool

- If your rolling tool is thicker than the one recommended, your bead will be larger and have a larger hole.
- If your rolling tool is thinner than the one recommended, your bead will be smaller and have a smaller hole.

Paper Thickness

- If your paper is thicker than the paper recommended in the materials list, use shorter paper strips.
- If your paper is thinner than the paper recommended in the materials list, use longer paper strips or layer 2-3 strips for each bead.

Remember, variations in size and shape can add a unique handmade element to your beads, so don't worry if all your beads aren't exactly the same.

TECHNIQUE LESSON

Painting Newspaper Beads

The following guide shows how to roll beads from newspaper, then finish with acrylic paint. It uses the **Paper Pearl Necklace** from page 16 as an example, but the technique is used for several other projects in the book.

Materials

For the paper beads
- Newspaper
- Acrylic paint in pearl white

For the necklace
- 144 bronze seed beads
- Two gold bead tips
- Two small seed beads (to be used inside the bead tips)
- Two 4 mm gold open jump rings
- One gold toggle clasp
- 107 in (270 cm) of 0.29 mm nylon beading thread

Tools
- Glue
- Toothpick
- Coating agent
- Flat nose pliers
- Round nose pliers

Paper Bead Chart

Paper Type	Paint Color	Strips to Cut	Number of Beads	Finished Size	Rolling Tool
Newspaper	Pearl white	290 isosceles triangles	145	About ¼ in (7 mm)	Toothpick

How to Make the Paper Beads

1. Cut the paper strips as noted in the diagram at right (also refer to the Paper Bead Chart above). Note that millimeters are the measurement units used in the diagram. If you'd prefer to work in inches, conversions are provided at right.

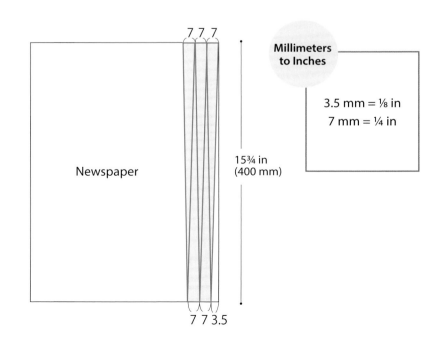

7 7 7

Millimeters to Inches

3.5 mm = ⅛ in
7 mm = ¼ in

15¾ in (400 mm)

Newspaper

7 7 3.5

2. Each bead uses two strips, so you'll need to cut 290 strips for a total of 145 beads. Group the strips in sets of two in preparation for rolling the beads.

3. Layer two strips, then roll the bead using a toothpick (refer to page 42). Note: It's alright if the strips have slightly different lengths at the end.

4. Glue the ends of the strips to the bead.

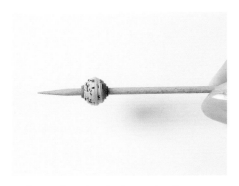

5. Once the glue is dry, twist the toothpick to remove the bead.

6. Coat the bead with acrylic paint.

7. Once the paint dries, apply a coating agent.

8. Repeat steps 3-7 to make a total of 145 beads.

How to Make the Necklace

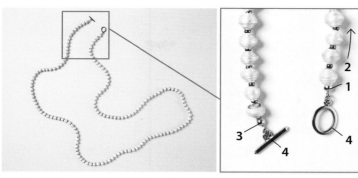

Finished Size: 48¼ in (122.5 cm)

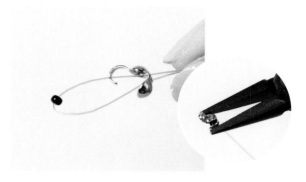

1. Start the necklace with a bead tip: String a small seed bead onto the center of the nylon thread, then fold the thread in half. Insert both strands through a bead tip. Use flat nose pliers to close the bead tip around the seed bead.

2. String the beads: Alternate between the paper beads and the bronze seed beads, stringing the beads onto both strands of the thread.

3. Finish the necklace with another bead tip: Insert both strands of thread through the remaining bead tip. String a small seed bead onto one strand of thread. Tie the thread in a knot, then apply a dab of glue. Use flat nose pliers to close the bead tip around the seed bead. Trim the excess threads on the outside of the bead tip.

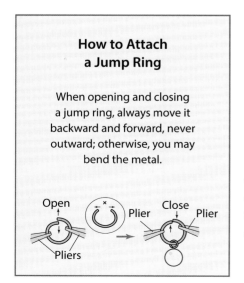

How to Attach a Jump Ring

When opening and closing a jump ring, always move it backward and forward, never outward; otherwise, you may bend the metal.

4. Install the clasp: Use round nose pliers to curl the hook on each bead tip. Attach a jump ring to each bead tip, as shown in the diagram at left. Attach the toggle clasp bar to one jump ring and the toggle clasp ring to the other before closing the jump rings.

TECHNIQUE LESSON

Coloring Beads with Marker

Use markers to decorate plain paper with hand-drawn designs and create one-of-a-kind beads. The following guide illustrates how to make striped beads by coloring the edges of the paper strips before rolling them. It uses the **Nautical Necklace & Bracelet** from page 24 as an example.

Materials

Necklace
For the paper beads
- One 8½ x 11 in (22 x 28 cm) sheet of drawing paper in each ivory, gray, blue, and yellow
- Blue marker

For the necklace
- One 10 mm brass open jump ring
- Four 8 mm brass twisted jump rings
- One 13 x 16 mm brass anchor charm
- One ⅝ in (16.5 mm) gold button

- 39½ in (100 cm) of 3 mm diameter gold rope
- Blue thread

Bracelet
For the paper beads
- One 8½ x 11 in (22 x 28 cm) sheet of drawing paper in each ivory, gray, and yellow
- Blue, mint green, and beige markers

For the bracelet
- One 6 mm brass open jump ring
- One 14 x 18 mm brass wheel charm

- 19¾ in (50 cm) of 0.7 mm stretchable nylon beading cord

Tools
- Glue
- Chopstick
- Coating agent
- Flat nose pliers
- Round nose pliers

Paper Bead Chart

	Bead	Paper Type	Paper Color	Strips to Cut	Number of Beads	Finished Size	Rolling Tool
Necklace	a	Drawing paper	Ivory with blue marker edges	3 isosceles triangles	3	About 1¼ in (30 mm)	Chopstick
	b		Yellow	6 isosceles triangles	6	About ¼ in (5 mm)	
	c-1		Gray	6 trapezoids	6	About ¼ in (7 mm)	
	c-2		Blue	6 trapezoids	6		
Bracelet	a		Ivory with blue, mint green, and beige marker edges (2 of each color)	6 isosceles triangles	6	About 1¼ in (30 mm)	
	c-1		Gray	4 trapezoids	4	About ¼ in (7 mm)	
	c-2		Yellow	3 trapezoids	3		

How to Make the Paper Beads

1. Cut the paper strips as noted in the diagrams below (also refer to the Paper Bead Chart on page 48). Note that millimeters are the measurement units used in the diagrams. If you'd prefer to work in inches, conversions are provided below.

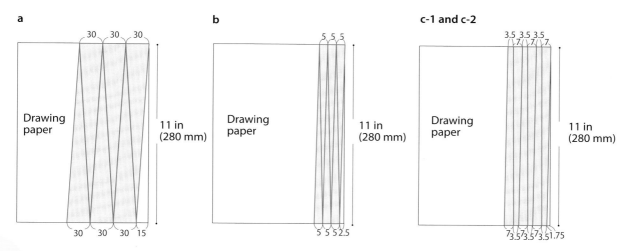

a

30 30 30

Drawing paper

11 in (280 mm)

30 30 30 15

b

5 5 5

Drawing paper

11 in (280 mm)

5 5 5 2.5

c-1 and c-2

3.5 3.5 3.5
7 7 7 7

Drawing paper

11 in (280 mm)

3.5 3.5 3.5 3.5 1.75

Millimeters to Inches

1.75 mm = ⅟₁₆ in
2.5 mm = ⅟₁₆ in
3.5 mm = ⅛ in
5 mm = ¼ in
7 mm = ¼ in
15 mm = ⅝ in
30 mm = 1¼ in

2. To make the a beads, use a marker to color the edges of the paper strips. Color three strips blue for the necklace. Color two strips each blue, mint green, and beige for the bracelet.

3. Roll the beads using a chopstick, then secure with a dab of glue (refer to page 42 for basic technique).

4. Apply a coating agent.

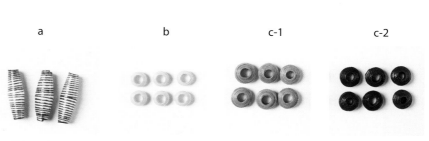

a   b   c-1   c-2

5. Roll beads b, c-1, and c-2. This photo shows the beads for the necklace. For the bracelet, you'll need six a beads (two of each color), four c-1 beads (gray), and three c-2 beads (yellow).

How to Make the Necklace

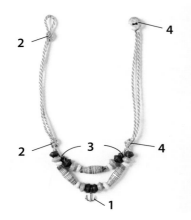

2

4

2

3

4

1

Finished Size: 17 in (43 cm)

1. Open the 10 mm jump ring and attach the anchor charm, then close the jump ring (refer to page 47 for instructions on attaching a jump ring).

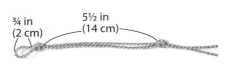

¾ in (2 cm)   5½ in (14 cm)

2. Fold the rope in half. Make a single knot (see page 60) ¾ in (2 cm) from the fold to create a button loop. Make another single knot 5½ in (14 cm) away.

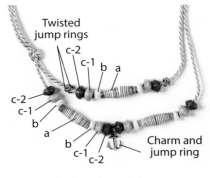

Twisted jump rings

c-2
c-1
b   a
c-2
c-1
b
a
b
c-1 c-2
Charm and jump ring

3. String the beads and the jump rings onto the two strands of rope, following the layout shown in the photo.

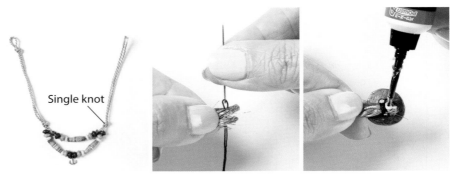

Single knot

4. Make a single knot using both strands at the end of the beads. Use the blue thread to sew the button to the rope ends. Apply a dab of glue on the wrong side of the button to secure in place.

How to Make the Bracelet

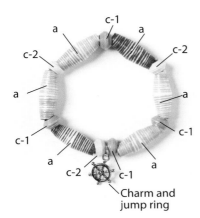

c-1
a   a
c-2   c-2
a   a
c-1   c-1
a   a
c-2   c-1
Charm and jump ring

Finished Size: 5¾ in (14.5 cm)

1. Attach the 6 mm jump ring to the wheel charm, following the same process used in step 1 of the necklace instructions shown above.

2. String the beads and jump ring onto the nylon cord, following the layout shown in the photo. Insert the nylon cord through the beads and jump ring again so they are double strung.

3. Knot the ends of the nylon cord three times. Apply a dab of glue to the knot. Trim the excess cord, leaving short ends.

4. Hide the cord ends by inserting them through a few beads.

Refer to the Two-Tone Bracelet on page 62 for more detailed instructions of steps 2-4.

TECHNIQUE LESSON

Making Beads with Washi Tape

Available in a wide variety of colors and patterns, washi tape is a wonderful material for bead making—simply cover plain paper with the tape before cutting your strips. The following guide shows how to make washi tape beads and how to attach grommets to beads for increased strength and style. The guide uses the **Rose Gold & Pink Pendant & Earrings** on page 18 as an example, but both the washi tape and grommet techniques are used for several other projects in the book.

Materials

Pendant
For the paper beads
- One 8½ x 11 in (22 x 28 cm) sheet of copy paper
- ⅝ in (1.5 cm) wide washi tape in peach, gold, and white stripe
- Two 3 mm gold grommets

For the pendant
- Eight 2 x 4 mm pink oval beads
- One 4.5 mm gold open jump ring
- 8 in (20 cm) of 26 gauge Artistic Wire in non-tarnish brass
- One 39½ in (100 cm) long gold chain

Earrings
For the paper beads
- One 8½ x 11 in (22 x 28 cm) sheet of copy paper
- ⅝ in (1.5 cm) wide washi tape in peach, gold, and white stripe
- Four 3 mm gold grommets

For the earrings
- 16 2 x 4 mm pink oval beads
- 16 in (40 cm) of 26 gauge Artistic Wire in non-tarnish brass
- Two gold hook earwires

Tools
- Glue
- Bamboo skewer
- Coating agent
- Flat nose pliers
- Round nose pliers
- Nipper pliers

Paper Bead Chart

	Paper Type	Paper Color	Strips to Cut	Number of Beads	Finished Size	Rolling Tool
Pendant	Copy paper	Adhere peach, gold, and white striped washi tape	1 trapezoid	1	About ⅝ in (15 mm)	Bamboo skewer
Earrings			2 trapezoids	2		

How to Make the Paper Beads

1. Adhere strips of washi tape to the copy paper. You don't need to cover the entire sheet of paper for this project. The photo shows enough tape for one bead.

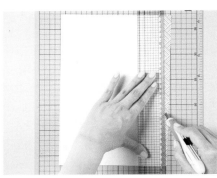

2. Cut the paper strips as noted in the diagram at right (also refer to the Paper Bead Chart on page 51). Note that millimeters are the measurement units used in the diagram. If you'd prefer to work in inches, conversions are provided below.

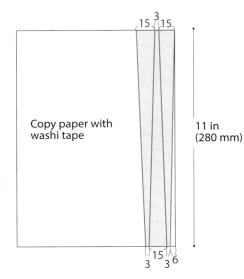

Copy paper with washi tape

11 in (280 mm)

15 3 15

3 15 3 6

Millimeters to Inches

3 mm = ⅛ in
6 mm = ¼ in
15 mm = ⅝ in

3. Use a bamboo skewer to curl the paper strip before rolling. Next, use the bamboo skewer to roll the bead (refer to page 42 for basic technique). Note: You may need to apply a few dabs of glue to hold the bead together as you roll since the combination of tape and paper can be a bit thick.

4. Secure the end with a dab of glue.

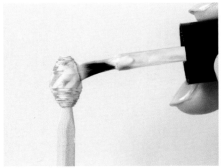

5. Apply a coating agent.

6. Place a grommet on a bamboo skewer. Apply a couple dabs of glue to the grommet.

7. Insert the paper bead onto the grommet.

8. Use the same process to glue another grommet to the other end of the bead.

About Grommets

Also called eyelets, grommets are ring-shaped metal components that are commonly used for attaching bag handles or shoelaces. They are composed of two parts: a grommet and a washer. You can use grommets designed specifically for crafts, but I prefer to use electronic grommets. These small grommets are usually less than 3 mm in diameter and feature longer tubes. No matter which type you buy, you'll use only the grommet, which is the part with the tube. Attaching grommets to a paper bead helps to secure and support the bead's hole. Plus, they allow you to string a paper bead onto hard materials, such as wires and pins.

How to Make the Pendant

Finished Size: 48¼ in (122.5 cm)

1. String the oval beads onto the center of an 8 in (20 cm) long piece of wire.

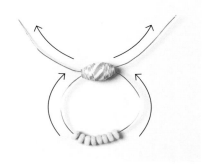

2. Insert the wire ends through the paper bead crosswise.

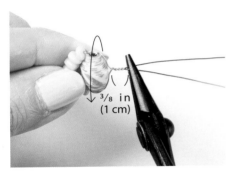

3. Hold the wire with flat nose pliers. Rotate the bead, twisting the wire for ⅜ in (1 cm).

4. Wrap the twisted wire around round nose pliers to form a loop.

5. Wrap the wire ends around the loop twice. Trim the excess wire using nipper pliers.

6. Completed view of the pendant.

7. Open the jump ring and attach the pendant and chain (refer to page 47 for instructions on attaching jump rings).

8. Close the jump ring.

How to Make the Earrings

Finished Size: ¾ x 1¼ in (2 x 3 cm)

Follow steps 1-6 on page 53 and above to make a pendant for each earring. Attach a hook earwire to each pendant loop.

TECHNIQUE LESSON

Making Beads with Small Pieces of Paper

Small pieces of paper, such as wine labels, candy wrappers, and postage stamps can be used for bead making—you'll just need to attach them to larger pieces of paper first. The following guide shows how to connect multiple strips of paper to create a bead featuring a wine label for the **Leather Cord Bracelet** on page 32.

Materials

For the paper beads
- One 1½ x 4¾ in (3.6 x 12 cm) section of a wine label
- One 8½ x 11 in (22 x 28 cm) sheet of drawing paper in each lime green and gray

For the bracelet
- 12 in (33 cm) of 2 mm diameter leather cord in each gold, copper, and bronze
- One 5 mm gold open jump ring
- Two 6 mm gold open jump rings
- Four 11 mm gold twisted jump rings
- One 12 x 16 mm gold starfish charm
- One gold hook clasp set with glue-in ends
  —Hook: 10 x 17.5 mm with a 4 x 6.5 mm inside diameter
  —Eye: 8 x 10.5 mm with a 4 x 6.5 mm inside diameter

Tools
- Glue
- Paintbrush (or other rolling tool with a 7 mm diameter handle)
- Coating agent
- Pliers

Paper Bead Chart

Paper Type	Paper Color	Strips to Cut	Number of Beads	Finished Size	Rolling Tool
Wine label	White print	6 rectangles			
Drawing paper	Lime green	3 rectangles	3 combined	About ¼ in (6 mm)	Paintbrush
	Gray	3 rectangles			

This side view of the finished bead shows the three layers of paper used to construct the bead. Since the leather cords used for this bracelet are pretty thick, you'll need a rolling instrument with a large diameter. Look for a paintbrush or marker with a 7 mm diameter.

How to Make the Paper Beads

1. Cut the paper strips as noted in the diagrams below (also refer to the Paper Bead Chart on page 55). Note that millimeters are the measurement units used in the diagrams. If you'd prefer to work in inches, conversions are provided below.

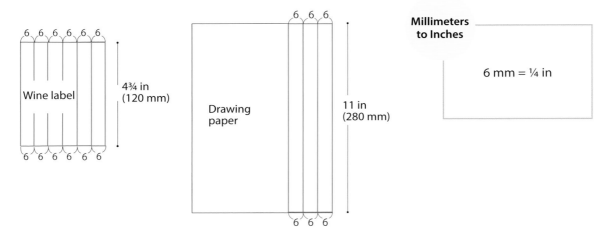

Millimeters to Inches

6 mm = ¼ in

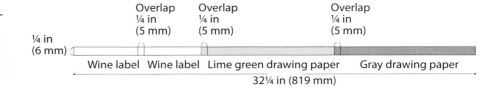

2. Use glue to connect strips of the wine label, lime green drawing paper, and gray drawing paper, as shown in the diagram at right.

Note: Position the wine labels with the wrong side facing up. The printed side should be visible once the bead is rolled.

3. Starting at the end with the gray paper, roll the bead using a paintbrush with a 7 mm diameter (refer to page 42 for basic technique).

4. Secure the end with a dab of glue.

5. Apply a coating agent, making sure to cover the top and bottom of the bead in addition to the sides. Make two more beads.

How to Make the Bracelet

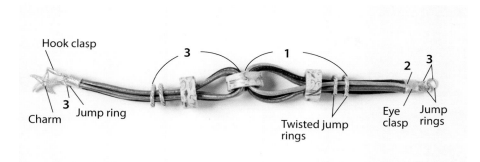

Finished Size: 7 in (18 cm)

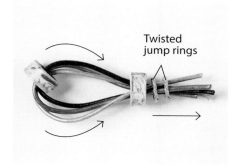

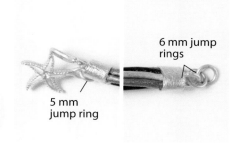

1. Cut each piece of leather cord in half. String a paper bead onto the center of three cords (use one of each color). Fold the cords in half, then string another paper bead and two twisted jump rings onto all six strands.

2. Tape the six strands of cord together with a small piece of tape. Apply a dab of glue to the bundled cords, then insert into the eye clasp.

3. Insert the remaining three leather cords through the first paper bead strung in step 1. Repeat the rest of step 1 and step 2 to complete the other half of the bracelet. Attach the 5 mm jump ring and charm to the hook clasp, then attach the two 6 mm jump rings to the eye clasp (refer to page 47 for instructions on attaching jump rings).

Ombré Bracelets

Shown on page 6

Finished Size:
7½ in (19 cm)

Materials

For the paper beads
Bracelet A
- One 8½ x 11 in (22 x 28 cm) sheet of copy paper printed with a pink and white design (see page 38 for a photo of the paper used in this bracelet)
- One 8½ x 11 in (22 x 28 cm) sheet each of drawing paper in pink and purple
- One 8½ x 11 in (22 x 29 cm) sheet of periwinkle blue tracing paper

Bracelet B
- One 8½ x 11 in (22 x 28 cm) sheet of copy paper printed with a blue and white design (see page 38 for a photo of the paper used in this bracelet)
- One 8½ x 11 in (22 x 28 cm) sheet each of drawing paper in blue and bright blue

- 2 x 11¾ in (5 x 30 cm) of blue and silver wrapping paper or recycled packaging (see page 39 for a photo of the paper used in this bracelet)

For the bracelets
Bracelet A
- 12 in (30 cm) each of DMC No. 25 embroidery floss in purple (#3835), pink (#153), and blue (#799)
- 19¾ in (50 cm) of 0.7 mm stretchable nylon beading cord

Bracelet B
- 12 in (30 cm) each of DMC No. 25 embroidery floss in bright blue (#791), navy (#3842), and blue gray (#931)
- 19¾ in (50 cm) of 0.7 mm stretchable nylon beading cord

Tools
- Glue
- Bamboo skewer
- Coating agent

Paper Bead Chart

Bracelet	Bead	Paper Type	Paper Color	Strips to Cut	Number of Beads	Finished Size	Rolling Tool
A	a	Copy paper	Pink and white print	4 isosceles triangles	4	About ⅜ in (10 mm)	Bamboo skewer
	b	Drawing paper	Pink		4		
	c		Purple	5 isosceles triangles	5		
	d	Tracing paper	Periwinkle blue	6 isosceles triangles	6		
B	a	Copy paper	Blue and white print	4 isosceles triangles	4	About ⅜ in (10 mm)	Bamboo skewer
	b	Drawing paper	Blue		4		
	c	Wrapping paper or recycled packaging	Blue and silver print	5 isosceles triangles	5		
	d	Drawing paper	Bright blue		5		

How to Make the Paper Beads

1. Cut the paper strips as noted in the diagram below (also refer to the Paper Bead Chart on page 58). Note that millimeters are the measurement units used in the diagram. If you'd prefer to work in inches, conversions are provided below.

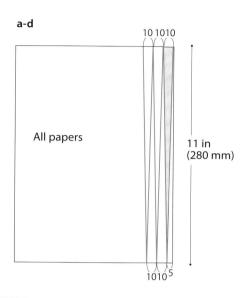

a-d

10 10 10

All papers

11 in
(280 mm)

1010 5

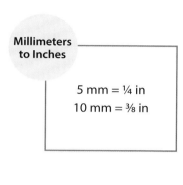

Millimeters to Inches

5 mm = ¼ in

10 mm = ⅜ in

---

2. Roll the beads using a bamboo skewer, then secure with a dab of glue (refer to page 42 for basic technique).

Bamboo skewer

3. Apply a coating agent to the beads.

How to Make the Bracelets

1. String the beads onto the nylon cord. Insert the nylon cord through the beads again so they are double strung.

2. Knot the ends of the nylon cord three times. Apply a dab of glue to the knot. Trim the excess cord, leaving short ends.

3. Hide the cord ends by inserting them through a few beads.

4. Cut each piece of embroidery floss in half to create two 6 in (15 cm) pieces for each color.

5. Fold the pieces of embroidery floss in half and loop them around the bracelet.

6. Make a single knot, as shown below.

7. Trim the embroidery floss ¾–1 in (2–2.5 cm) from the knot.

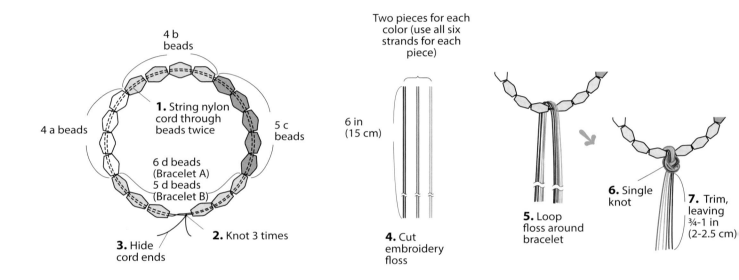

4 b beads

4 a beads

1. String nylon cord through beads twice

5 c beads

6 d beads (Bracelet A)
5 d beads (Bracelet B)

3. Hide cord ends

2. Knot 3 times

Two pieces for each color (use all six strands for each piece)

6 in (15 cm)

4. Cut embroidery floss

5. Loop floss around bracelet

6. Single knot

7. Trim, leaving ¾-1 in (2-2.5 cm)

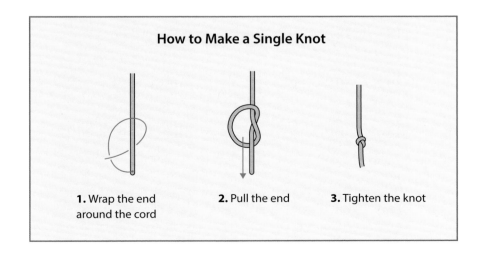

How to Make a Single Knot

1. Wrap the end around the cord

2. Pull the end

3. Tighten the knot

Two-Tone Bracelets

Shown on page 7

A

B

Finished Size:
7 in (18 cm)

Materials

For the paper beads
Bracelet A
- One 8½ x 11 in (22 x 28 cm) sheet each of drawing paper in white and turquoise

Bracelet B
- One 8½ x 11 in (22 x 28 cm) sheet each of drawing paper in white and purple

For the bracelets (both A and B)
- 19¾ in (50 cm) of 0.7 mm stretchable nylon beading cord

Tools
- Glue
- Bamboo skewer
- Coating agent

Paper Bead Chart

Bracelet	Bead	Paper Type	Paper Color	Strips to Cut	Number of Beads	Finished Size	Rolling Tool
A	a	Drawing paper	White	6 isosceles triangles	6	About ⅜ in (10 mm)	Bamboo skewer
	b		Turquoise	12 isosceles triangles	12		
B	a	Drawing paper	White	6 isosceles triangles	6	About ⅜ in (10 mm)	Bamboo skewer
	b		Purple	12 isosceles triangles	12		

How to Make the Paper Beads

1. Cut the paper strips as noted in the diagram at right (also refer to the Paper Bead Chart above). Note that millimeters are the measurement units used in the diagram. If you'd prefer to work in inches, conversions are provided at right.

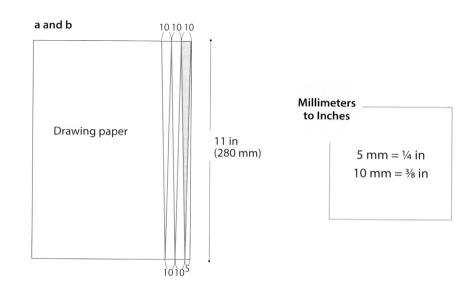

a and b

10 10 10

Drawing paper

11 in (280 mm)

10 10 5

Millimeters to Inches

5 mm = ¼ in
10 mm = ⅜ in

2. Roll the beads using a bamboo skewer, then secure with a dab of glue (refer to page 42 for basic technique).

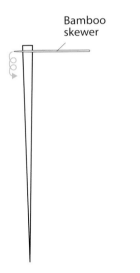

Bamboo skewer

3. Apply a coating agent to the beads.

How to Make the Bracelets

1. String the beads onto the nylon cord. Insert the nylon cord through the beads again so they are double strung.

2. Knot the ends of the nylon cord three times. Apply a dab of glue to the knot. Trim the excess cord, leaving short ends.

3. Hide the cord ends by inserting them through a few beads.

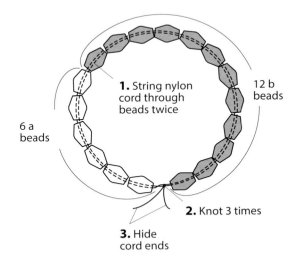

6 a beads

1. String nylon cord through beads twice

12 b beads

2. Knot 3 times

3. Hide cord ends

Lemonade Necklace

Shown on page 8

Finished Size:
51¼ in (130 cm)

Materials

For the paper beads
- One 8½ x 11 in (22 x 28 cm) sheet of light blue drawing paper
- One 8½ x 11 in (22 x 28 cm) sheet of gray drawing paper
- Two 8½ x 11 in (22 x 28 cm) sheets of yellow floral print washi paper

For the necklace
- 57 in (145 cm) each of DMC No. 25 embroidery floss in light blue (#775), gray (#169), and yellow (#834)

Tools
- Glue
- Bamboo skewer
- Coating agent
- Beading needle

Washi is a traditional Japanese paper made from specific native plants. Known for its strength, flexibility, and lightness, washi paper has been used for centuries.

Paper Bead Chart

Bead	Paper Type	Paper Color	Strips to Cut	Number of Beads	Finished Size	Rolling Tool
a	Drawing paper	Light blue	36 isosceles triangles	36	About ⅜ in (10 mm)	Bamboo skewer
b		Gray	14 isosceles triangles	14		
c	Washi paper	Yellow floral print	48 isosceles triangles	48		

How to Make the Paper Beads

1. Cut the paper strips as noted in the diagram below (also refer to the Paper Bead Chart above). Note that millimeters are the measurement units used in the diagram. If you'd prefer to work in inches, conversions are provided below.

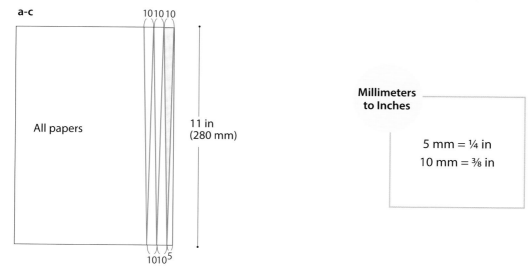

a-c

10 10 10

All papers

11 in
(280 mm)

10 10 5

Millimeters to Inches

5 mm = ¼ in
10 mm = ⅜ in

2. Roll the beads using a bamboo skewer, then secure with a dab of glue (refer to page 42 for basic technique).

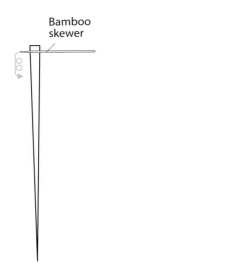

Bamboo skewer

3. Apply a coating agent to the beads.

How to Make the Necklace

1. Thread a beading needle with the three pieces of embroidery floss (use all six strands for each piece).

2. Tape the floss to your work surface 9¾ in (25 cm) from the end. String the beads onto the floss, stopping at the tape (refer to the diagram on page 65 for bead layout).

3. Make a single knot at the end of the beads (see page 60). Remove the tape and make another knot, right next to the beads.

4. Work a 7 in (17.5 cm) three-strand braid at each end (see page 65).

5. Make a single knot at the end of each braid.

6. Trim the ends to ¼ in (7 mm).

1. Thread needle with embroidery floss

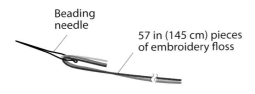

Beading needle

57 in (145 cm) pieces of embroidery floss

2. Tape floss to surface and string beads

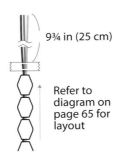

9¾ in (25 cm)

Refer to diagram on page 65 for layout

3. Make single knot to secure beads

4. 7 in (17.5 cm) three-strand braid

6. Trim

¼ in (7 mm)

5. Single knot

¼ in (7 mm)

5. **6.**

18 a beads

18 a beads

48 c beads

7 b beads

7 b beads

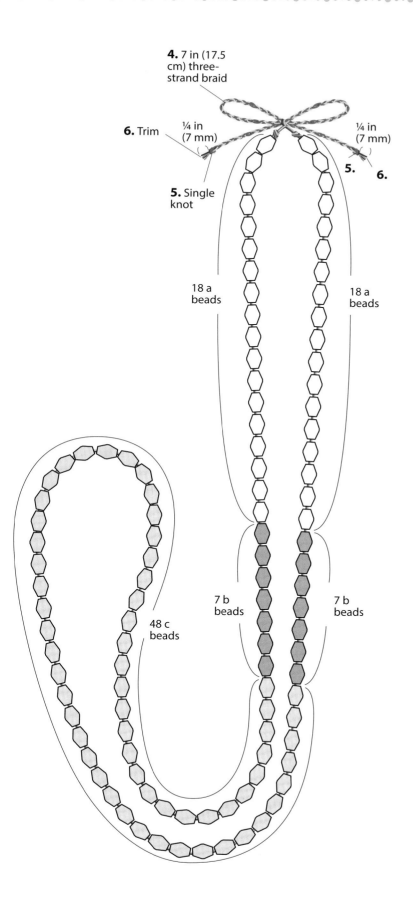

How to Make a Three-Strand Braid

A B C

1. Cross A over B

B A C

2. Cross C over A

B C A

3. Continue braiding by bringing the outside cords to the center

4. Tighten the braid as you work

Pastel Confetti Necklace & Bracelets

Shown on page 10

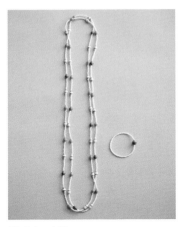

Finished Size:
Necklace: 78¾ in (200 cm)
Bracelets: 6 in (15 cm)

Materials

Necklace
For the paper beads
- One 8½ x 11 in (22 x 28 cm) sheet each of drawing paper in pink, purple, blue, and multicolor stripe

For the necklace
- 780 small white beads
- 86½ in (220 cm) of No. 3 nylon beading cord

Bracelets (for one bracelet)
For the paper beads
- One 8½ x 11 in (22 x 28 cm) sheet of drawing paper in blue, pink, or purple

For the bracelets
- 82 small white beads
- 9¾ in (25 cm) of 0.7 mm stretchable nylon beading cord

Tools
- Glue
- Bamboo skewer
- Coating agent

Paper Bead Chart

	Bead	Paper Type	Paper Color	Strips to Cut	Number of Beads	Finished Size	Rolling Tool
Necklace	a	Drawing paper	Pink	9 isosceles triangles	9	About ⅜ in (10 mm)	Bamboo skewer
	b		Purple	8 isosceles triangles	8		
	c		Blue	9 isosceles triangles	9		
	d		Multicolor stripe	26 isosceles triangles	26	About ½ in (13 mm)	
Bracelet	e	Drawing paper	Blue	2 isosceles triangles	1	About ⅜ in (10 mm)	Bamboo skewer
	f		Pink		1		
	g		Purple		1		

How to Make the Paper Beads for the Necklace

1. Cut the paper strips as noted in the diagram below (also refer to the Paper Bead Chart on page 66). Note that millimeters are the measurement units used in the diagram. If you'd prefer to work in inches, conversions are provided below.

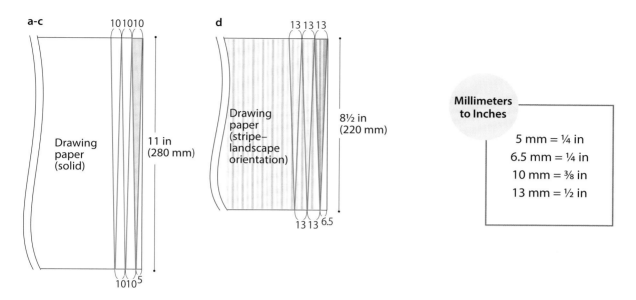

a–c

10 10 10

Drawing paper (solid)

11 in (280 mm)

10 10 5

d

13 13 13

Drawing paper (stripe– landscape orientation)

8½ in (220 mm)

13 13 6.5

Millimeters to Inches

5 mm = ¼ in
6.5 mm = ¼ in
10 mm = ⅜ in
13 mm = ½ in

---

2. Roll the beads using a bamboo skewer, then secure with a dab of glue (refer to page 42 for basic technique).

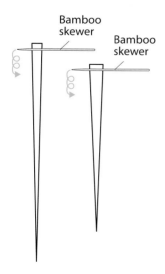

Bamboo skewer

Bamboo skewer

3. Apply a coating agent to the beads.

How to Make the Necklace

1. String the beads onto the nylon cord (refer to the diagram for bead layout).

2. Knot the ends of the nylon cord three times. Apply a dab of glue to the knot. Trim the excess cord, leaving short ends.

3. Hide the cord ends by inserting them through a few beads.

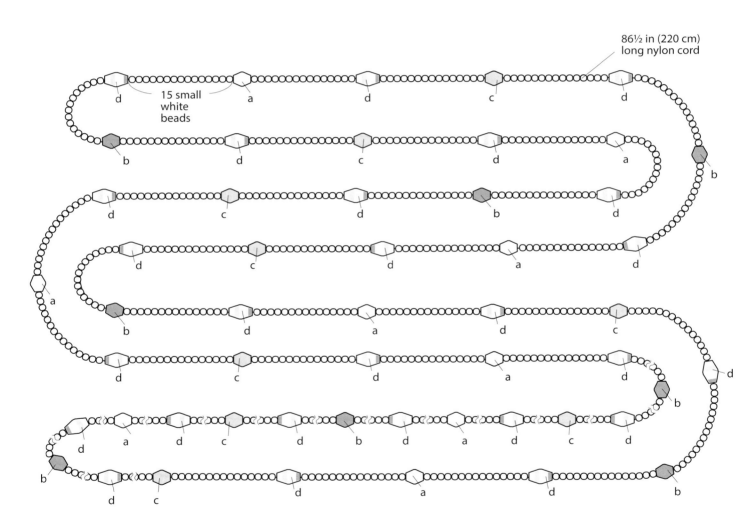

How to Make the Paper Bead for the Bracelet

1. Cut the paper strips as noted in the diagram below (also refer to the Paper Bead Chart on page 66). Note that millimeters are the measurement units used in the diagram. If you'd prefer to work in inches, conversions are provided below.

e-g

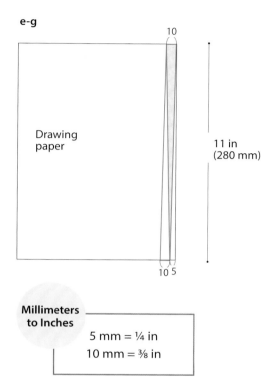

Drawing paper

10

11 in (280 mm)

10 5

Millimeters to Inches

5 mm = ¼ in

10 mm = ⅜ in

2. Layer two strips. Roll the bead using a bamboo skewer, then secure with a dab of glue (refer to steps 3 and 4 on page 46 for tips on rolling beads with two strips).

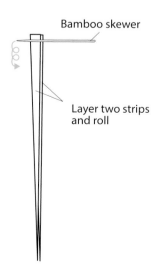

Bamboo skewer

Layer two strips and roll

3. Apply a coating agent to the bead.

How to Make the Bracelets

1. String the beads onto the stretchable nylon cord (refer to the diagram for bead layout).

2. Knot the ends of the nylon cord three times. Apply a dab of glue to the knot. Trim the excess cord, leaving short ends.

3. Hide the cord ends by inserting them through a few beads.

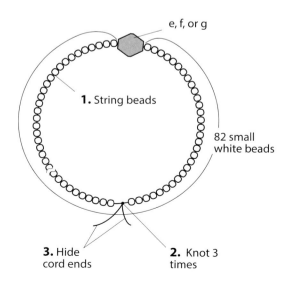

e, f, or g

1. String beads

82 small white beads

3. Hide cord ends

2. Knot 3 times

Floret Necklace

Shown on page 12

Finished Size:
26¾ in (68 cm)

Materials

For the paper beads
- 11¾ x 16½ in (30 x 42 cm) piece of green and white print wrapping or scrapbook paper

For the necklace
- 14 6 mm round green onyx beads
- 14 6 mm Czech fire-polished pink glass beads
- Two 6 x 8 mm rondelle antique gold metal beads
- 32 4 mm round antique gold metal beads
- Two 39½ in (100 cm) long pieces of DMC No. 25 embroidery floss in teal (#3847)

Tools
- Glue
- Bamboo skewer
- Coating agent
- Beading needle

Paper Bead Chart

Bead	Paper Type	Paper Color	Strips to Cut	Number of Beads	Finished Size	Rolling Tool
a	Wrapping/ scrapbook paper	Green and white print	7 double trapezoids	7	About 1 in (25 mm)	Bamboo skewer
b			7 isosceles triangles	7	About ⅝ in (17 mm)	

How to Make the Paper Beads

1. Cut the paper strips as noted in the diagram below (also refer to the Paper Bead Chart above). Note that millimeters are the measurement units used in the diagram. If you'd prefer to work in inches, conversions are provided below.

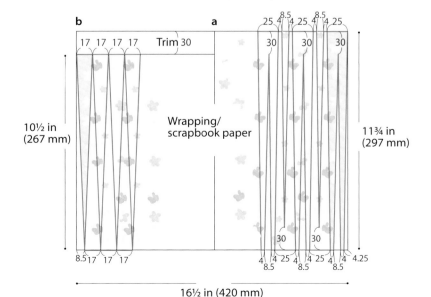

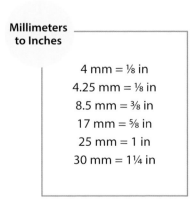

Millimeters to Inches

4 mm = ⅛ in
4.25 mm = ⅛ in
8.5 mm = ⅜ in
17 mm = ⅝ in
25 mm = 1 in
30 mm = 1¼ in

2. Roll the beads using a bamboo skewer, then secure with a dab of glue (refer to page 42 for basic technique).

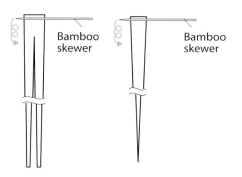

Bamboo skewer

Bamboo skewer

3. Apply a coating agent to the beads.

How to Make the Necklace

1. Make the outer strand: String beads onto one piece of embroidery floss (use all six strands).

2. Make the inner strand: String beads onto the other piece of embroidery floss (use all six strands).

3. Use a beading needle to insert both pieces of embroidery floss through a rondelle metal bead and two round metal beads at each end of the necklace.

4. Align the two pieces of embroidery floss so they are equal in length. Make a single knot next to the final bead at each end of the necklace (see page 60).

5. At each end of the necklace, divide the embroidery floss into three groups of four strands each. Work the three-strand braid for 6¾ in (17 cm) at each end (see page 65).

6. Make a single knot at each end.

7. Trim the ends

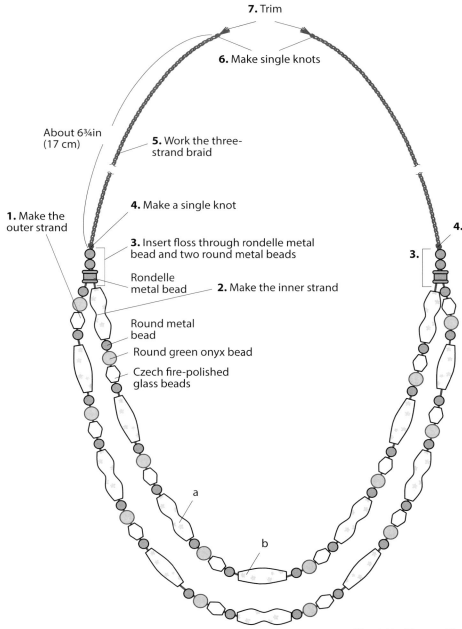

7. Trim

6. Make single knots

About 6¾in (17 cm)

5. Work the three-strand braid

4. Make a single knot

1. Make the outer strand

3. Insert floss through rondelle metal bead and two round metal beads

Rondelle metal bead

2. Make the inner strand

Round metal bead

Round green onyx bead

Czech fire-polished glass beads

4.

3.

a

b

Golden Deco Necklace

Shown on page 14

Materials

For the paper beads
- 11¾ x 15¾ in (30 x 40 cm) pieces of wrapping paper in gold and white

For the necklace
- 117 small gold beads
- Two gold bead tips
- Two crimp beads (to be used inside the bead tips)

- Two 4.5 mm gold open jump rings
- One gold toggle clasp
- 78¾ in (200 cm) of 0.7 mm stretchable nylon beading cord

Tools
- Glue
- Bamboo skewer
- Coating agent
- Flat nose pliers
- Round nose pliers

Finished Size:
67 in (170 cm)

Paper Bead Chart

Bead	Paper Type	Paper Color	Strips to Cut	Number of Beads	Finished Size	Rolling Tool
a	Wrapping paper	White	31 isosceles triangles	31	About 1½ in (35 mm)	Bamboo skewer
b		Gold	9 isosceles triangles	9		

How to Make the Paper Beads

1. Cut the paper strips as noted in the diagram below (also refer to the Paper Bead Chart above). Note that millimeters are the measurement units used in the diagram. If you'd prefer to work in inches, conversions are provided below.

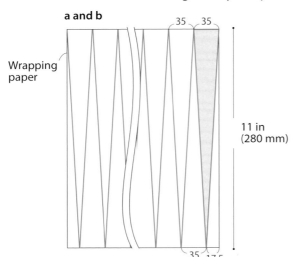

a and b

Wrapping paper

35 35

11 in (280 mm)

35 17.5

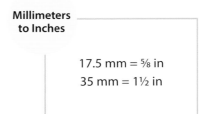

Millimeters to Inches

17.5 mm = ⅝ in
35 mm = 1½ in

2. Roll the beads using a bamboo skewer, then secure with a dab of glue (refer to page 42 for basic technique).

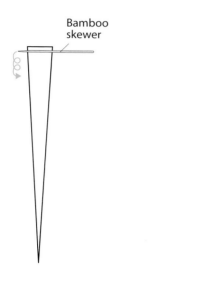

Bamboo
skewer

3. Apply a coating agent to the beads.

How to Make the Necklace

1. String a bead tip and crimp bead onto the stretchable nylon cord. Install the bead tip as shown on page 85.

2. String the beads onto the cord (refer to the diagram on page 74 for bead layout).

3. Install the remaining bead tip and crimp bead at the end of the necklace.

4. Install the clasp as shown in step 4 on page 47.

1. Install bead tip at beginning of cord

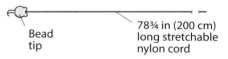

Bead
tip

78¾ in (200 cm)
long stretchable
nylon cord

2. String beads

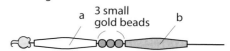

a   3 small
gold beads   b

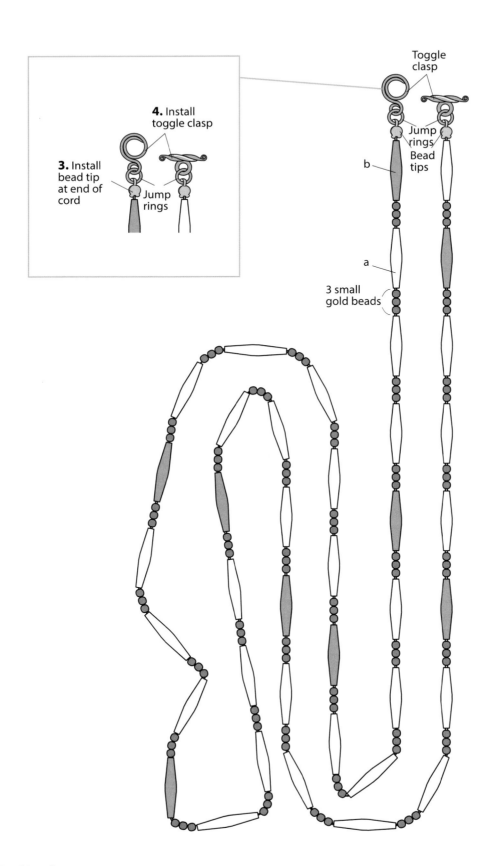

4. Install toggle clasp

3. Install bead tip at end of cord

Jump rings

Toggle clasp

Jump rings

Bead tips

b

a

3 small gold beads

Braided Flowers Bracelet & Ring

Shown on page 19

Finished Size:
Bracelet: 9½ in (24 cm)
Ring: ¾ in (2 cm)

Materials

Bracelet
For the paper beads
- 11 x 17 in (28 x 43 cm) piece of gray and white floral print wrapping paper
- One 8½ x 11 in (22 x 28 cm) sheet each of drawing paper in gray, light gray, and pink

For the bracelet
- Eight 6 mm pink barrel-shaped Czech glass beads
- Four 4 mm clear pink fire-polished Czech glass beads
- 34 3 mm round bronze beads
- One 5 mm gold metal fastener
- 11¾ in (30 cm) of 2 mm flat suede cord in gray
- 31½ in (80 cm) of No. 3 nylon beading cord

Ring
For the paper beads
- 11 x 17 in (28 x 43 cm) piece of gray and white floral print wrapping paper
- One 8½ x 11 in (22 x 28 cm) sheet each of drawing paper in gray, light gray, and pink

For the ring
- Two 6 mm pink barrel-shaped Czech glass beads
- One 4 mm clear pink fire-polished Czech glass bead
- 25 3 mm round bronze beads
- 23¾ in (60 cm) of No. 3 nylon beading cord

Tools
- Glue
- Bamboo skewer
- Coating agent

Paper Bead Chart

	Bead	Paper Type	Paper Color	Strips to Cut	Number of Beads	Finished Size	Rolling Tool
Bracelet	a	Wrapping paper	Gray and white floral print	7 trapezoids	7	About ⅜ in (8 mm)	Bamboo skewer
	b	Drawing paper	Gray		7		
	c		Light gray		7		
	d		Pink		7		
Ring	a	Wrapping paper	Gray and white floral print	1 trapezoid	1	About ⅜ in (8 mm)	Bamboo skewer
	b	Drawing paper	Gray		1		
	c		Light gray		1		
	d		Pink		1		

How to Make the Paper Beads

1. Cut the paper strips as noted in the diagrams below (also refer to the Paper Bead Chart on page 75). Note: You'll only need half a sheet of each color of drawing paper. Note that millimeters are the measurement units used in the diagrams. If you'd prefer to work in inches, conversions are provided below.

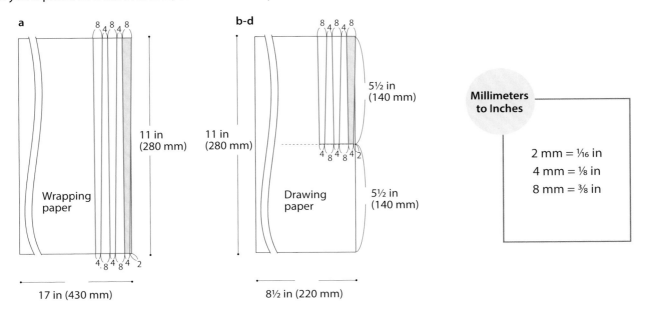

a

8 4 8 4 8

11 in (280 mm)

Wrapping paper

4 8 4 8 4 2

17 in (430 mm)

b-d

8 4 8 4 8

11 in (280 mm)

5½ in (140 mm)

4 8 4 8 2

Drawing paper

5½ in (140 mm)

8½ in (220 mm)

Millimeters to Inches

2 mm = ¹⁄₁₆ in

4 mm = ⅛ in

8 mm = ⅜ in

---

2. Roll the beads using a bamboo skewer, then secure with a dab of glue (refer to page 42 for basic technique).

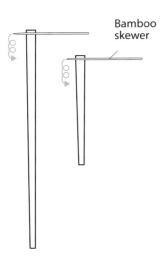

Bamboo skewer

3. Apply a coating agent to the beads

How to Make the Bracelet

1. Fold the nylon cord in half. String the beads, starting at the center of the cord (refer to the diagram for bead layout).

2. Knot the cord three times. Apply a dab of glue to the knot.

3. Align the two cord ends. Insert the cord ends through a few beads to hide the knot. Trim the excess cord.

4. Loop 6 in (15 cm) pieces of suede cord through each end of the bracelet.

5. Make a single knot in each piece of suede cord (refer to page 60).

6. Insert the four strands of suede cord through the metal fastener.

7. Make a single knot at the end of each cord set.

8. Trim the ends at an angle.

1. String the beads

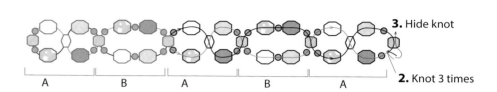

1. String the beads

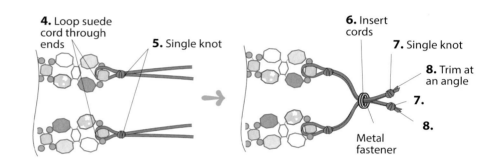

3. Hide knot

2. Knot 3 times

4. Loop suede cord through ends

5. Single knot

6. Insert cords

7. Single knot

8. Trim at an angle

7.

8.

Metal fastener

How to Make the Ring

1. Fold the nylon cord in half. String the beads, starting at the center of the cord (refer to the diagram for bead layout).

2. Insert the cord ends through the starting bead again to form into a ring.

3. To complete the ring, follow steps 2 and 3 of the bracelet instructions listed above.

1. String the beads

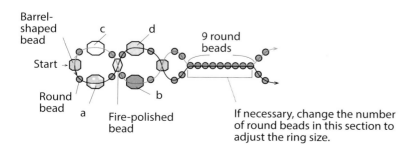

Barrel-shaped bead

Start

Round bead

a

c

d

b

Fire-polished bead

9 round beads

If necessary, change the number of round beads in this section to adjust the ring size.

2. Insert cord ends through starting bead

3. Refer to steps 2 and 3 above

Tassel Necklace, Pendant & Earrings

Shown on page 20

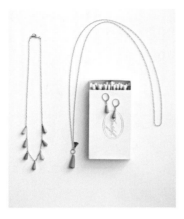

Finished Size:
Necklace: 16½ in (42 cm)
Pendant: 33½ in (85 cm)
Earrings: 1¼ in (3.2 cm)

Materials

Necklace
For the paper beads
- Newspaper
- Acrylic paint in turquoise, yellow, gold, pink, and fuchsia
- 14 2 x 2.5 mm gold grommets
- Seven 1¼ in (30 mm) gold ball tip headpins

For the necklace
- Two 4 mm gold open jump rings
- One gold lobster clasp
- One 5 x 7 mm gold chain tab
- One 15¾ in (40 cm) gold chain

Pendant
For the paper beads
- Newspaper
- Acrylic paint in turquoise
- Two 2 x 2.5 mm gold grommets
- One 1¼ in (30 mm) gold ball tip headpin

For the pendant
- One 8 x 10 mm gold fan charm
- One 8 mm gold open jump ring
- Two 4 mm gold open jump rings
- One 33½ in (85 cm) gold chain

Earrings
For the paper beads
- Newspaper
- Acrylic paint in turquoise
- Four 2 x 2.5 mm gold grommets
- Two 1¼ in (30 mm) gold ball tip headpins

For the earrings
- Two 3 mm gold open jump rings
- One set of gold lever-back earring findings

Tools
- Glue
- Toothpick
- Bamboo skewer
- Coating agent
- Round nose pliers
- Flat nose pliers
- Nipper pliers

Paper Bead Chart

	Bead	Paper Type	Paint Color	Strips to Cut	Number of Beads	Finished Size	Rolling Tool
Necklace	a	Newspaper	Turquoise	3 right triangles	3	About ⅜ in (10 mm)	Toothpick
	b		Yellow	1 right triangle each	1		
	c		Gold		1		
	d		Pink		1		
	e		Fuchsia		1		
Pendant	f	Newspaper	Turquoise	2 right triangles	1	About ¾ in (20 mm)	Bamboo skewer
Earrings	g	Newspaper	Turquoise	2 right triangles	2	About ⅜ in (10 mm)	Toothpick

How to Make the Paper Beads

1. Cut the paper strips as noted in the diagrams below (also refer to the Paper Bead Chart on page 78). Note that millimeters are the measurement units used in the diagrams. If you'd prefer to work in inches, conversions are provided below.

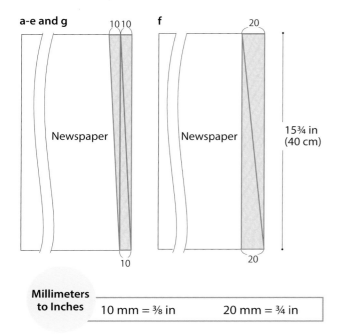

a-e and g

f

10 10

20

Newspaper

Newspaper

15¾ in (40 cm)

10

20

Millimeters to Inches

10 mm = ⅜ in   20 mm = ¾ in

2. Roll the beads using a toothpick or bamboo skewer as noted on page 78, then secure with a dab of glue (refer to page 42 for basic technique). Refer to steps 3 and 4 on page 46 for tips on rolling beads with two strips.

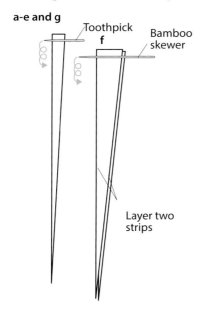

a-e and g

Toothpick

f

Bamboo skewer

Layer two strips

3. Coat the beads with acrylic paint. Allow the paint to dry, then twist the toothpick to remove the bead.

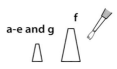

a-e and g   f

4. Apply a coating agent to the beads.

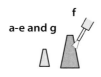

f

a-e and g

5. Glue a grommet to each end of each bead.

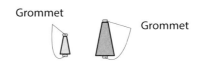

Grommet   Grommet

6. Insert a headpin into each paper bead and make a loop as shown on page 85.

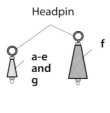

Headpin

a-e and g   f

How to Make the Necklace

1. Attach the paper beads to the chain: Starting at the center of the chain, attach the headpin loops to the chain every ¾ in (2 cm) as shown in the diagrams below.

2. Use jump rings to attach the lobster clasp and chain tab to the necklace.

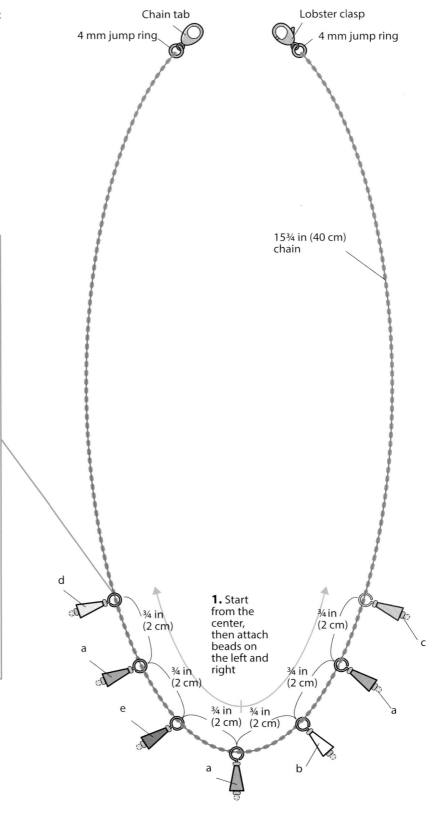

2. Attach clasp and tab

Chain tab

Lobster clasp

4 mm jump ring

4 mm jump ring

15¾ in (40 cm) chain

d

a

e

c

a

a

b

¾ in (2 cm)

¾ in (2 cm)

¾ in (2 cm)

¾ in (2 cm)

¾ in (2 cm)

¾ in (2 cm)

1. Start from the center, then attach beads on the left and right

Attach Paper Beads to Chain

1. Use flat nose pliers to open the loop and attach it to the chain (use same method as opening a jump ring as shown on page 47).

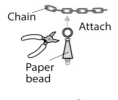

Chain

Attach

Paper bead

2. Use nipper pliers to close the loop.

How to Make the Pendant

1. Attach one of the 4 mm jump rings at the center of the chain (refer to page 47).

2. Attach the fan charm to the other 4 mm jump ring.

3. Open the 8 mm jump ring. Add the 4 mm jump ring with the fan charm from step 2 and paper bead f. Attach the 8 mm jump ring to the 4 mm jump ring on the chain, then close.

How to Make the Earrings

1. Attach a paper bead g to each 3 mm jump ring.

2. Attach each jump ring to an earring finding.

Earring finding

3 mm jump ring

g

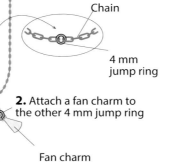

33½ in (85 cm) chain

1. Attach a 4 mm jump ring to center of chain

Chain

4 mm jump ring

3. Attach the 8 mm jump ring to the 4 mm jump ring on the chain

2. Attach a fan charm to the other 4 mm jump ring

Fan charm

f

Aquamarine Necklace & Earrings

Shown on page 22

Finished Size:
Necklace: 17 in (43 cm)
Earrings: 1½ in (4 cm) from base
of hook

Materials

Necklace
For the paper beads
- One 8½ x 11 in (22 x 28 cm) sheet of white copy paper
- One 8½ x 11 in (22 x 28 cm) sheet of mint drawing paper
- ⅝ in (1.5 cm) wide silver and mint print washi tape

For the necklace
- 26 5 mm charcoal gray pearls
- 96 4 mm charcoal gray pearls
- 15 2½ in (65 mm) silver headpins
- Two 4 mm silver open jump rings
- One 3 x 4 mm silver chain tab
- One silver lobster clasp
- Two silver bead tips
- Two 2 mm crimp beads (to be used inside the bead tips)
- 23¾ in (60 cm) of No. 3 nylon beading cord

Earrings
For the paper beads
- One 8½ x 11 in (22 x 28 cm) sheet of white copy paper
- ⅝ in (1.5 cm) wide silver and mint print washi tape

For the earrings
- Four 4 mm charcoal gray pearls
- Two 2½ in (65 mm) silver headpins
- Four 4 mm silver open jump rings
- Two 20 mm silver hook earwires

Tools
- Glue
- Toothpick
- Bamboo skewer
- Coating agent
- Round nose pliers
- Flat nose pliers
- Nipper pliers

Paper Bead Chart

	Bead	Paper Type	Paper Color	Strips to Cut	Number of Beads	Finished Size	Rolling Tool
Necklace	a	Copy paper	Adhere silver and mint washi tape	5 trapezoids	5	About 1¼ in (30 mm)	Bamboo skewer
	b			4 trapezoids	4	About 1½ in (40 mm)	
	c	Drawing paper	Mint	3 trapezoids	3	About 1¼ in (30 mm)	
	d				3	About 1½ in (40 mm)	
Earrings	e	Copy paper	Adhere silver and mint washi tape	2 trapezoids	2	About 1¼ in (30 mm)	Bamboo skewer

How to Make the Paper Beads

1. Adhere strips of washi tape to the white copy paper, without leaving any gaps. Cut the paper strips as noted in the diagram below (also refer to the Paper Bead Chart on page 82). Note that millimeters are the measurement units used in the diagram. If you'd prefer to work in inches, conversions are provided below.

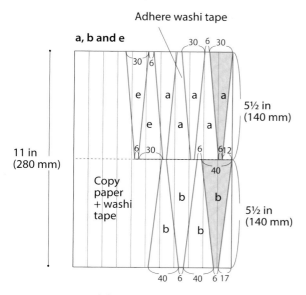

a, b and e

Adhere washi tape

5½ in (140 mm)

5½ in (140 mm)

11 in (280 mm)

Copy paper + washi tape

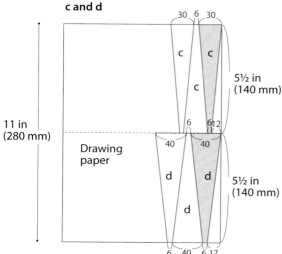

c and d

5½ in (140 mm)

5½ in (140 mm)

11 in (280 mm)

Drawing paper

Millimeters to Inches

6 mm = ¼ in
12 mm = ½ in
17 mm = ⅝ in
30 mm = 1¼ in
40 mm = 1½ in

2. Roll the beads using a bamboo skewer, then secure with a dab of glue (refer to page 42 for basic technique).

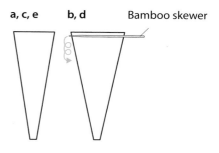

a, c, e   b, d   Bamboo skewer

3. Apply a coating agent to the beads.

4. String two 4 mm pearls and a paper bead onto each headpin, then make a loop as shown on page 85.

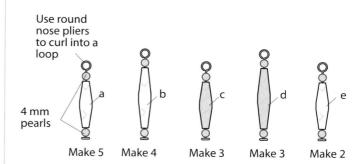

Use round nose pliers to curl into a loop

4 mm pearls

a   b   c   d   e

Make 5   Make 4   Make 3   Make 3   Make 2

How to Make the Necklace

1. String a bead tip and crimp bead onto the nylon cord. Install the bead tip as shown on page 85.

2. String the first 39 pearls onto the cord (refer to the diagram for bead layout).

3. Alternately string the headpins and 5 mm pearls onto the nylon cord (refer to the diagram for bead layout).

4. String the remaining pearls onto the cord (refer to the diagram for bead layout).

5. Install the remaining bead tip and crimp bead at the end of the necklace.

6. Use the jump rings to install the lobster clasp and chain tab (refer to page 47 for instructions on attaching jump rings).

1. Install bead tip at beginning of cord

Bead tip

23¾ in (60 cm) long
nylon cord

If necessary, use an eyeleteer
to widen the pearl holes
before stringing onto the cord.

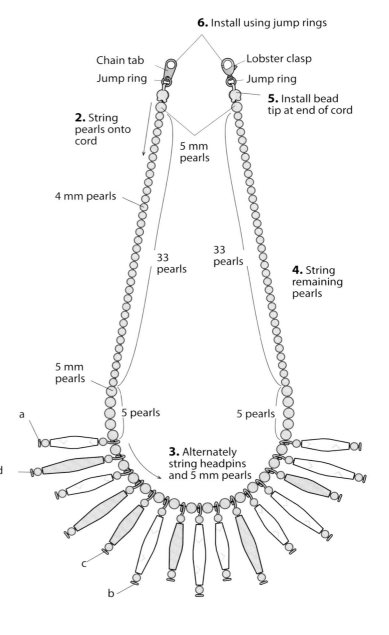

6. Install using jump rings

Chain tab
Jump ring

Lobster clasp
Jump ring

5. Install bead tip at end of cord

2. String pearls onto cord

5 mm pearls

4 mm pearls

33 pearls

33 pearls

4. String remaining pearls

5 mm pearls

5 pearls

5 pearls

3. Alternately string headpins and 5 mm pearls

a

d

c

b

How to Make the Earrings

1. Prepare two headpins with e beads and 4 mm pearls, as noted in step 4 on page 83.

2. Use two jump rings to attach each headpin to a hook earwire (refer to page 47 for instructions on attaching jump rings).

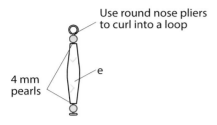

Use round nose pliers to curl into a loop

4 mm pearls

e

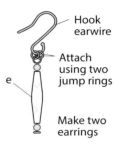

Hook earwire

Attach using two jump rings

e

Make two earrings

How to Install a Bead Tip Using a Crimp Bead

This guide is for attaching bead tips on one strand of nylon cord. Refer to page 47 for instructions on working with a double strand.

Crimp bead

Nylon cord

1. String the bead tip and crimp bead onto the cord. Use flat nose pliers to squeeze the crimp bead.

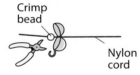

2. Apply a dab of glue.

Flat nose pliers

Trim

3. Use flat nose pliers to close the bead tip around the crimp bead. Trim the excess cord.

How to Make Pin Loops

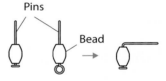

Pins

Bead

1. String a bead onto the pin. Use round nose pliers to bend the pin at a 90° angle.

¼ in (6-7 mm)

2. Trim the pin about ¼ in (6-7 mm) from the bead.

Round nose pliers

3. Hold the end of the pin with round nose pliers. Rotate your wrist to curl the pin around the tip of the pliers.

To connect the pin to other components, follow the same process used for attaching jump rings as shown on page 47.

Glam Garnet Necklace

Shown on page 26

Finished Size:
17¼ in (44 cm)

Materials

For the paper beads
- One sheet of newspaper
- Acrylic paint in gold, blue, and plum
- 18 2 x 2.5 mm gold grommets

For the necklace
- 15 6 mm round blue frosted beads
- Nine 8 mm textured gold open jump rings
- 11 4 mm gold open jump rings
- Nine 1¼ in (30 mm) gold ball tip headpins
- Two ⅝ in (17 mm) gold three-strand end bars
- One 7 x 19 mm gold toggle clasp
- Six gold bead tips
- Six crimp beads (to be used inside the bead tips)
- 11¾ in (30 cm) gold chain
- 17¾ in (45 cm) of 0.7 mm stretchable nylon beading cord

Tools
- Glue
- Bamboo skewer
- Coating agent
- Flat nose pliers
- Round nose pliers
- Nipper pliers

Paper Bead Chart

Bead	Paper Type	Paint Color	Strips to Cut	Number of Beads	Finished Size	Rolling Tool
a		Gold	13 isosceles triangles	13	About ¼ in (7 mm)	
b	Newspaper	Blue	10 rectangles	10	About ⅜ in (8 mm)	Bamboo skewer
c		Plum	18 isosceles triangles	9	About ⅜ in (10 mm)	

How to Make the Paper Beads

1. Cut the newspaper strips as noted in the diagrams below (also refer to the Paper Bead Chart above). Note that millimeters are the measurement units used in the diagrams. If you'd prefer to work in inches, conversions are provided below.

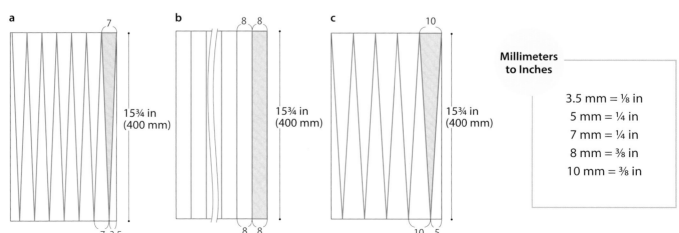

Millimeters to Inches

3.5 mm = ⅛ in
5 mm = ¼ in
7 mm = ¼ in
8 mm = ⅜ in
10 mm = ⅜ in

2. Roll the beads using a bamboo skewer, then secure with a dab of glue. Refer to steps 3 and 4 on page 46 for tips on rolling beads with two strips.

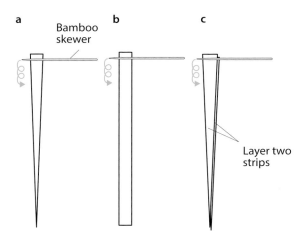

a

b

c

Bamboo skewer

Layer two strips

3. Coat the beads with acrylic paint. Allow the paint to dry, then twist the toothpick to remove the bead.

4. Apply a coating agent to the beads.

5. Glue a grommet to each end of each paper bead c. Refer to steps 6 and 7 on pages 52 and 53 for tips on attaching grommets to beads.

Grommet

6. Insert a headpin into each paper bead c and make a loop as shown on page 85.

Headpin

How to Make the Necklace

1. Strands 1-3 are all made the same way, but feature different bead layouts. To start each strand, string a bead tip and crimp bead onto a 6 in (15 cm) long piece of stretchable nylon cord. Install the bead tip as shown on page 85. String the beads onto the cord (refer to the diagram below for bead layouts). Install another bead tip and crimp bead at the end of the strand.

2. Use round nose pliers to curl the hook of each bead tip (refer to step 4 on page 47).

3. Use six 4 mm jump rings to attach the bead tips to the end bars, assembling strands 1-3.

4. Use a 4 mm jump ring to attach the chain to one end bar.

5. Use two 4 mm jump rings to attach the toggle clasp ring to the other end bar.

6. Use two 4 mm jump rings to attach the toggle clasp bar to the end of the chain.

1. Make strands 1-3

Strands 1-3 begin and end with bead tips, but feature different bead layouts. Refer to page 85 for instructions on installing a bead tip using a crimp bead.

Bead tip

6 in (15 cm) long stretchable nylon cord

String beads

Attach a bead tip at the other end

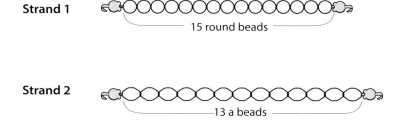

Strand 1

15 round beads

Strand 2

13 a beads

Strand 3

b

8 mm jump ring

Attach the jump ring to the pin loop (refer to page 47)

9 c beads on pins

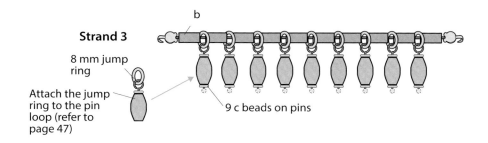

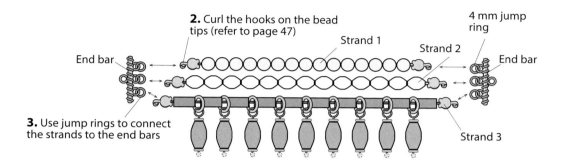

2. Curl the hooks on the bead tips (refer to page 47)

Strand 1

Strand 2

4 mm jump ring

End bar

End bar

3. Use jump rings to connect the strands to the end bars

Strand 3

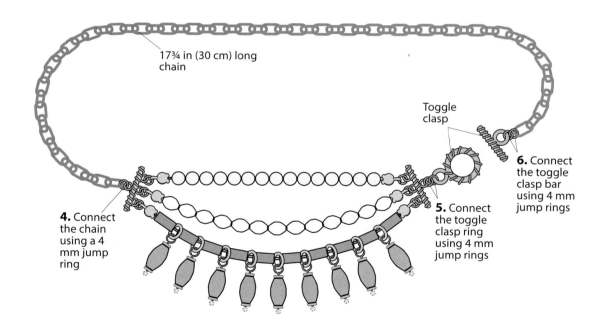

17¾ in (30 cm) long chain

Toggle clasp

4. Connect the chain using a 4 mm jump ring

5. Connect the toggle clasp ring using 4 mm jump rings

6. Connect the toggle clasp bar using 4 mm jump rings

Festive Friendship Bracelet A

Shown on page 28

Materials

For the paper beads
- One 8½ x 11 in (22 x 28 cm) sheet each of drawing paper in orange, blue, and light blue

For the bracelet
- 47¼ in (120 cm) of 1 mm red waxed cord

Tools
- Glue
- Toothpicks
- Coating agent
- Beading needle

Finished Size:
8¼ in (21 cm)

Paper Bead Chart

Bead	Paper Type	Paper Color	Strips to Cut	Number of Beads	Finished Size	Rolling Tool
a		Orange	5 rectangles	5	About ¼ in (5 mm)	Toothpick
b	Drawing paper	Blue	5 rectangles	5		
c		Light blue	5 rectangles	5		

How to Make the Paper Beads

1. Cut the paper strips as noted in the diagram below (also refer to the Paper Bead Chart above). Note: It may help to fold the paper in thirds before measuring and cutting the strips. Note that millimeters are the measurement units used in the diagram. If you'd prefer to work in inches, conversions are provided below.

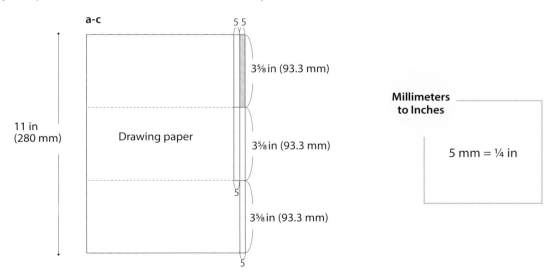

a-c

5 5

3⅝ in (93.3 mm)

11 in
(280 mm)

Drawing paper

3⅝ in (93.3 mm)

5

3⅝ in (93.3 mm)

5

Millimeters to Inches

5 mm = ¼ in

2. Roll the beads using a toothpick, then secure with a dab of glue (refer to page 42 for basic technique).

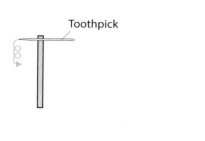

Toothpick

3. Apply a coating agent to the beads

How to Make the Bracelet

1. Thread a beading needle with the waxed cord. Fold the waxed cord in half so there are two strands.

2. Make a single knot 6 in (15 cm) from the fold (see page 60).

3. String a bead onto the cord. Make a single knot. Continue alternating between beads and knots (refer to the diagram below for bead layout).

4. Trim the cord ends 6 in (15 cm) from the final single knot.

5. Use the left cord ends to make an adjustable overhand knot around the right cord ends.

6. Make a single knot using both strands of the left cord ends.

7. Trim the excess cord.

8. Repeat steps 5-7 on the other side of the bracelet, using the right cord ends.

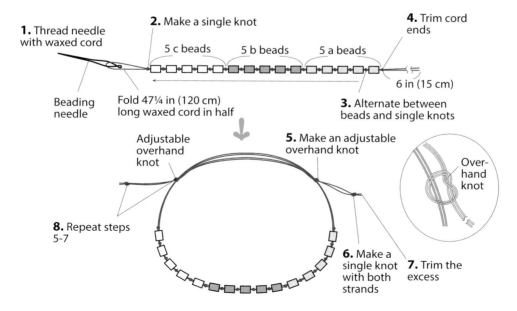

1. Thread needle with waxed cord

2. Make a single knot

5 c beads 5 b beads 5 a beads

4. Trim cord ends

Beading needle

Fold 47¼ in (120 cm) long waxed cord in half

3. Alternate between beads and single knots

6 in (15 cm)

Adjustable overhand knot

5. Make an adjustable overhand knot

Over-hand knot

8. Repeat steps 5-7

6. Make a single knot with both strands

7. Trim the excess

Festive Friendship Bracelet B

Shown on page 28

Finished Size:
8¼ in (21 cm)

Materials

For the paper beads
- One 8½ x 11 in (22 x 28 cm) sheet of copy paper printed with a light orange design

For the bracelet
- 33½ in (85 cm) of 1 mm blue waxed cord
- 27½ in (70 cm) of 2 mm yellow hemp cord

Tools
- Glue
- Bamboo skewer
- Coating agent
- Beading needle

Paper Bead Chart

Bead	Paper Type	Paper Color	Strips to Cut	Number of Beads	Finished Size	Rolling Tool
a	Copy paper	Light orange print	14 isosceles triangles	14	About ¼ in (7 mm)	Bamboo skewer

How to Make the Paper Beads

1. Cut the paper strips as noted in the diagram below (also refer to the Paper Bead Chart above). Note that millimeters are the measurement units used in the diagram. If you'd prefer to work in inches, conversions are provided below.

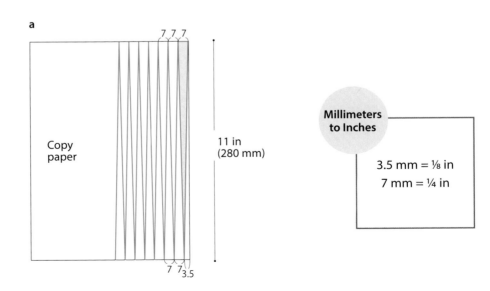

2. Roll the beads using a bamboo skewer, then secure with a dab of glue (refer to page 42 for basic technique).

Bamboo skewer

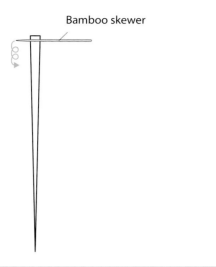

3. Apply a coating agent to the beads.

How to Make the Bracelet

1. Thread a beading needle with the hemp cord. Fold the hemp cord in half so there are two strands. String the beads onto the cord.

2. Cut a 19¾ in (50 cm) long piece of waxed cord. Tie the center of the waxed cord to the bracelet about 4 in (10 cm) from the folded end (right before the first bead). Follow the process shown on page 94 to make square knots between each bead.

3. Cross the hemp cord ends. Use the remaining 13¾ in (35 cm) long piece of waxed cord to make a square knot fastener composed of 2.5 square knots around the hemp cord ends (refer to page 94).

4. Make a single knot using both strands of the cord ends (see page 60).

5. Trim the excess cord.

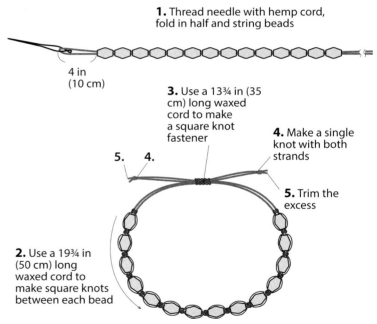

1. Thread needle with hemp cord, fold in half and string beads

3. Use a 13¾ in (35 cm) long waxed cord to make a square knot fastener

4. Make a single knot with both strands

5. Trim the excess

2. Use a 19¾ in (50 cm) long waxed cord to make square knots between each bead

4 in (10 cm)

5.　　4.

How to Make a Square Knot

Core cords

A   B

1. Bring A over the core cords and under B.

2. Bring B under the core cords and through the loop created by A.

3. Pull A and B sideways to tighten. Half of the square knot is now complete.

4. Fold A across the bracelet. Bring B over A, under the core cords, and through the loop created by A.

5. Pull A and B sideways to tighten. One square knot is now complete.

How to Make a Square Knot Fastener

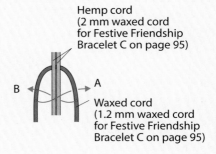

Hemp cord (2 mm waxed cord for Festive Friendship Bracelet C on page 95)

B   A

Waxed cord (1.2 mm waxed cord for Festive Friendship Bracelet C on page 95)

1. Fold the waxed cord in half and loop it around the hemp cord. Cross A and B as shown.

B   A

A   B

2. Pull A and B sideways to tighten. Cross A and B again, then tighten. One square knot is now complete.

2.5 square knots (2 square knots for Festive Friendship Bracelet C on page 95)

3. Make the specified number of square knots. Insert the cord ends under a few knots to secure, then trim the excess. Apply a dab of glue to the ends to secure.

Festive Friendship Bracelet C

Shown on page 28

Finished Size:
8¼ in (21 cm)

Materials

For the paper beads
- One 8½ x 11 in (22 x 28 cm) sheet of copy paper printed with a multicolor wave design
- Two 3.5 mm gold grommets

For the bracelet
- 31½ in (80 cm) of 2 mm red waxed cord

- 90½ in (230 cm) of 1 mm red waxed cord
- 78¾ in (200 cm) of 1 mm gray waxed cord

Tools
- Glue
- ⅛ in (3.5 mm) diameter knitting needle (US size 4) or dowel
- Coating agent

Paper Bead Chart

Bead	Paper Type	Paper Color	Strips to Cut	Number of Beads	Finished Size	Rolling Tool
a	Copy paper	Multicolor wave design	1 trapezoid	1	About 1¼ in (30 mm)	⅛ in (3.5 mm) diameter knitting needle or dowel

How to Make the Paper Bead

1. Cut the paper strip as noted in the diagram below (also refer to the Paper Bead Chart above). Note that millimeters are the measurement units used in the diagram. If you'd prefer to work in inches, conversions are provided below.

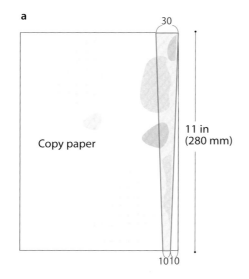

a

30

Copy paper

11 in (280 mm)

10 10

Millimeters to Inches

10 mm = ⅜ in

30 mm = 1¼ in

2. Roll the bead using a knitting needle or dowel, then secure with a dab of glue (refer to page 42 for basic technique).

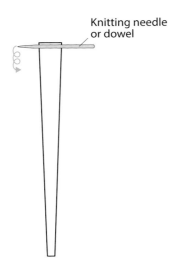

Knitting needle or dowel

3. Apply a coating agent to the bead.

4. Glue a grommet to each end of each bead. Refer to steps 6 and 7 on pages 52 and 53 for tips on attaching grommets to beads.

Grommet

How to Make the Bracelet

1. Cut the 31½ in (80 cm) long piece of 2 mm red waxed cord in half. String the paper bead onto both cords.

2. Cut 39½ in (100 cm) long pieces of the 1 mm red and gray waxed cords. Weave the 1 mm waxed cords around the 2 mm red waxed cords for 1¾ in (4.5 cm) as shown in the diagram on page 97.

3. Knot the 1 mm waxed cords twice, using the same process used to attach the cords. Apply a dab of glue to the knot, then trim the excess cord.

4. Repeat steps 2-3 on the other side of the paper bead.

5. Cross the 2 mm red waxed cord ends. Use the remaining 11¾ in (30 cm) long piece of 1 mm red waxed cord to make a square knot fastener composed of two square knots around the 2 mm red waxed cord ends (refer to page 94).

6. Make a single knot (see page 60) using both strands of the cord ends.

7. Trim the excess cord.

1. String the paper bead onto the cords

Two 15¾ in (40 cm) long pieces of 2 mm red waxed cord

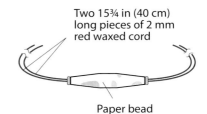

Paper bead

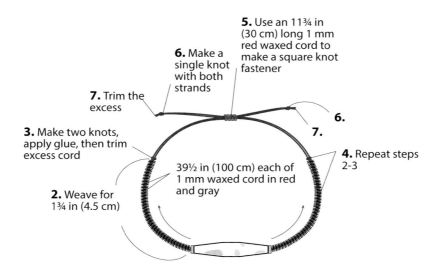

5. Use an 11¾ in (30 cm) long 1 mm red waxed cord to make a square knot fastener

6. Make a single knot with both strands

7. Trim the excess

3. Make two knots, apply glue, then trim excess cord

2. Weave for 1¾ in (4.5 cm)

39½ in (100 cm) each of 1 mm waxed cord in red and gray

6.

7.

4. Repeat steps 2-3

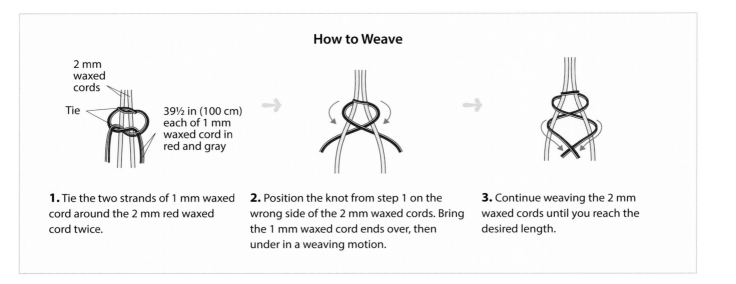

How to Weave

2 mm waxed cords

Tie

39½ in (100 cm) each of 1 mm waxed cord in red and gray

1. Tie the two strands of 1 mm waxed cord around the 2 mm red waxed cord twice.

2. Position the knot from step 1 on the wrong side of the 2 mm waxed cords. Bring the 1 mm waxed cord ends over, then under in a weaving motion.

3. Continue weaving the 2 mm waxed cords until you reach the desired length.

Boho Wrap Bracelets

Shown on page 29

Finished Size:
15¾ in (40 cm)

Materials

Bracelet A
For the paper beads
- 8½ x 11 in (22 x 28 cm) pieces of wrapping paper in green text print, orange text print, and multicolor floral print (see page 38 for photos of the papers used in this bracelet)

For the bracelet
- One 15 mm shell button
- 39½ in (100 cm) of 1.2 mm natural leather cord
- 137¾ in (350 cm) of brown Nymo nylon monocord

Bracelet B
For the paper beads
- 8½ x 11 in (22 x 28 cm) pieces of wrapping paper in white text print, blue text print, and multicolor floral print

For the bracelet
- One 15 mm shell button
- 39½ in (100 cm) of 1.2 mm natural leather cord
- 137¾ in (350 cm) of navy blue Nymo nylon monocord

Tools
- Glue
- Bamboo skewer
- Coating agent
- Beading needle

Paper Bead Chart

Bracelet	Bead	Paper Type	Paper Color	Strips to Cut	Number of Beads	Finished Size	Rolling Tool
A	a	Wrapping paper	Green text print	18 trapezoids each	18	About ¼ in (6 mm)	Bamboo skewer
	b		Multicolor floral print		18	About ¼ in (6 mm)	
	c		Orange text print		18	About ¼ in (6 mm)	
B	a	Wrapping paper	White text print	18 trapezoids each	18	About ¼ in (6 mm)	Bamboo skewer
	b		Multicolor floral print		18	About ¼ in (6 mm)	
	c		Blue text print		18	About ¼ in (6 mm)	

How to Make the Paper Beads

1. Cut the paper strips as noted in the diagrams below (also refer to the Paper Bead Chart on page 98). Note: It may help to fold the paper for the b beads in half before measuring and cutting the strips. Note that millimeters are the measurement units used in the diagrams. If you'd prefer to work in inches, conversions are provided below.

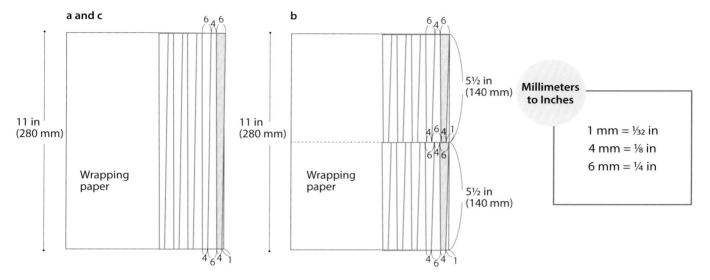

a and c

6 4 6

11 in
(280 mm)

Wrapping paper

4 6 4 1

b

6 4 6

11 in
(280 mm)

5½ in
(140 mm)

4 6 4 1

6 4 6

Wrapping paper

5½ in
(140 mm)

4 6 4 1

Millimeters to Inches

1 mm = 1/32 in

4 mm = 1/8 in

6 mm = 1/4 in

> Note: In this sample, the paper used for the b beads was significantly thicker than the paper used for beads a and c. The strip length was shortened for the b beads to ensure that all the beads would have similar finished sizes. Adjust your strip length accordingly based on the thickness of your paper (refer to page 44 for more details on how paper thickness effects finished bead size).

2. Roll the beads using a bamboo skewer, then secure with a dab of glue (refer to page 42 for basic technique).

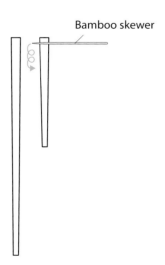

Bamboo skewer

3. Apply a coating agent to the beads.

How to Make the Bracelet

1. Fold the 39½ in (100 cm) long leather cord in half. String the shell button onto the center of the cord.

2. Make a single knot right after the button, using both strands of the leather cord (see page 60).

3. Fold the 137¾ in (350 cm) long monocord in half. Use the ladderwork technique shown in the guide below to attach the beads (refer to the diagram at right for bead layout).

4. Make a single knot using both strands of leather cord. Make another single knot 1 in (2.5 cm) away.

5. Make single knots in each individual strand of leather cord 1 in (2.5 cm) away from the knot made in step 4.

6. Trim each cord end at an angle, about ⅛ in (3 mm) from the knot.

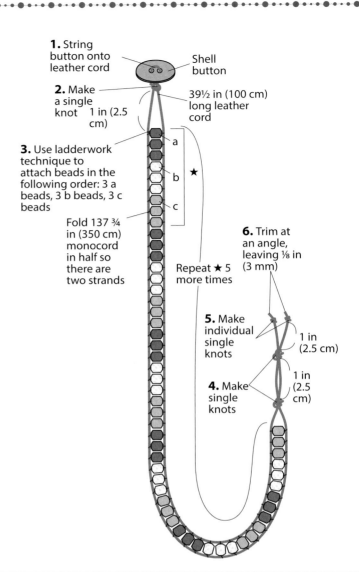

1. String button onto leather cord — Shell button

2. Make a single knot   1 in (2.5 cm)   39½ in (100 cm) long leather cord

3. Use ladderwork technique to attach beads in the following order: 3 a beads, 3 b beads, 3 c beads

a
b ★
c

Fold 137¾ in (350 cm) monocord in half so there are two strands

Repeat ★ 5 more times

6. Trim at an angle, leaving ⅛ in (3 mm)

5. Make individual single knots

4. Make single knots

1 in (2.5 cm)
1 in (2.5 cm)

The Ladderwork Technique

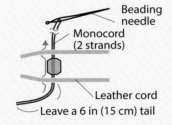

Beading needle
Monocord (2 strands)
Leather cord
Leave a 6 in (15 cm) tail

1. Thread the beading needle with monocord, then fold in half. String the first bead onto the monocord, positioning the monocord under the leather cords.

2. Loop the monocord over the outer leather cord, then insert back through the bead. Knot the monocord and thread tail together three times.

3. Follow the same process to string the next bead, first bringing the monocord under the leather cords, then back over the leather cords.

4. Repeat until all beads have been strung. To finish, knot the monocord around the leather cord three times. Pass the monocord back through the last 2-3 beads, then trim the excess. Use this same process to finish the thread tail from step 1.

Bangle Bracelet

Shown on page 30

Finished Size:
7 in (17.5 cm)

Materials

For the paper beads
- 6 x 11¾ in (15 x 30 cm) piece of gold wrapping paper or recycled food packaging
- 8½ x 11 in (22 x 28 cm) section of a map
- Six 2.5 mm gold grommets

For the bracelet
- Two 11 x 15 mm antique gold oval beads
- Two 2 x 8 mm gold rondelle beads
- One gold bangle bracelet with twist-off bead ends
- 8 in (20 cm) of 24 gauge Artistic Wire in non-tarnish brass

Tools
- Glue
- Bamboo skewer
- Coating agent

Paper Bead Chart

Bead	Paper Type	Paper Color	Strips to Cut	Number of Beads	Finished Size	Rolling Tool
a	Wrapping paper or recycled food packaging	Gold	4 isosceles triangles	1	About ¾ in (20 mm)	Bamboo skewer
b	Map	Map print	6 right triangles	2	About ¾ in (20 mm)	

How to Make the Paper Beads

1. Cut the paper strips as noted in the diagrams below (also refer to the Paper Bead Chart above). Note that millimeters are the measurement units used in the diagrams. If you'd prefer to work in inches, conversions are provided below.

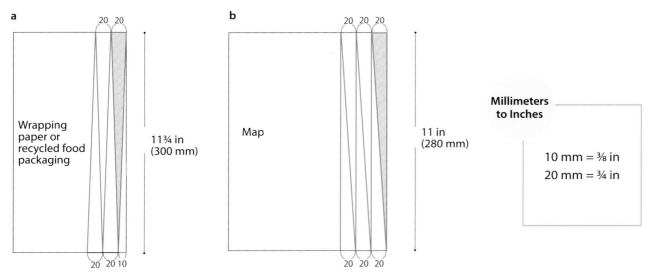

a

Wrapping paper or recycled food packaging

11¾ in (300 mm)

20 20

20 20 10

b

Map

11 in (280 mm)

20 20 20

20 20 20

Millimeters to Inches

10 mm = ⅜ in
20 mm = ¾ in

2. Roll the beads using a bamboo skewer, then secure with a dab of glue. Refer to steps 3 and 4 on page 46 for tips on rolling beads with multiple strips.

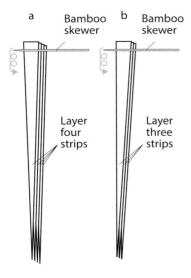

3. Apply a coating agent to the beads.

4. Glue a grommet to each end of each bead. Refer to steps 6 and 7 on pages 52 and 53 for tips on attaching grommets to beads.

How to Make the Bracelet

1. String the beads onto the bangle following the layout shown in the diagram below.

2. Wrap 4 in (10 cm) long pieces of wire around the bangle 5-6 times to secure the beads in place.

3. Glue the twist-off bead ends to the bangle.

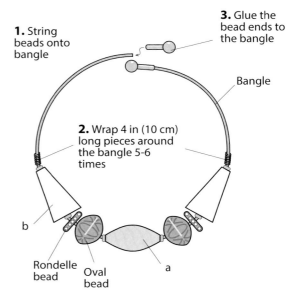

Chain Petite Necklace & Ribbon Bracelets

Shown on page 31

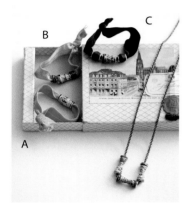

Finished Size:
Necklace: 34½ in (87.5 cm)
Bracelets: 6 in (15 cm)

Materials

Necklace
For the paper beads
- 4¾ x 12¼ in (12 x 31 cm) piece of yellow and pink print wrapping paper or recycled food packaging

For the necklace
- Two 5 mm black open jump rings
- One black lobster clasp
- One black extender chain
- 31½ in (80 cm) long black chain

Bracelet A
For the paper beads
- 2¾ x 12¼ in (7 x 31 cm) piece of blue print wrapping paper or recycled food packaging
- Two 4 mm gold grommets

For the bracelet
- 9¾ in (25 cm) of 16 mm wide stretch ribbon in blue

Bracelet B
For the paper beads
- 2¾ x 12¼ in (7 x 31 cm) piece of pink print wrapping paper or recycled food packaging

- One 4 mm gold grommet
- One 5 mm gold grommet

For the bracelet
- 9¾ in (25 cm) of 16 mm wide stretch ribbon in pink
- Six 8 mm antique gold twisted jump rings

Bracelet C
For the paper beads
- 2¾ x 12¼ in (7 x 31 cm) piece of black print wrapping paper or recycled food packaging
- One 2¾ x 12¼ in (7 x 31 cm) sheet of black drawing paper
- Five 4 mm gold grommets
- One 5 mm gold grommet

For the bracelet
- 9¾ in (25 cm) of 16 mm wide stretch ribbon in black

Tools
- Glue
- Chopstick (4-5 mm diameter)
- Coating agent
- Flat nose pliers

Paper Bead Chart

	Bead	Paper Type	Paper Color	Strips to Cut	Number of Beads	Finished Size	Rolling Tool
Necklace	a	Wrapping paper or recycled food packaging	Pink and yellow print	6 double right triangles	3	About ¾ in (20 mm)	Bamboo skewer
Bracelet A	b	Wrapping paper or recycled food packaging	Blue print	2 distorted trapezoids	1	About ¾ in (18 mm)	Chopstick
Bracelet B	c		Pink print	2 right triangles	1	About ⅝ in (15 mm)	
Bracelet C	d		Black print	2 right triangles	1	About ⅝ in (15 mm)	
	e	Drawing paper	Black	2 isosceles triangles	2	About ⅜ in (10 mm)	

How to Make the Paper Beads for the Necklace

1. Cut the paper strips as noted in the diagram below (also refer to the Paper Bead Chart above. Note that millimeters are the measurement units used in the diagram. If you'd prefer to work in inches, conversions are provided below.

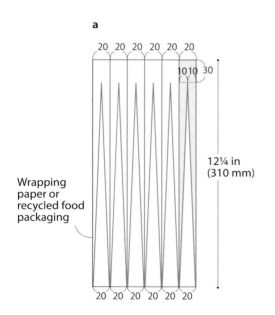

Millimeters to Inches

10 mm = ⅜ in
20 mm = ¾ in
30 mm = 1¼ in

2. Roll the beads using a bamboo skewer, then secure with a dab of glue. Refer to steps 3 and 4 on page 46 for tips on rolling beads with two strips.

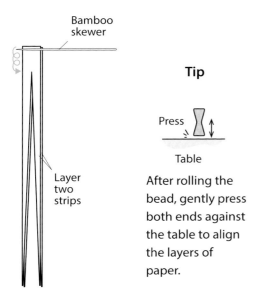

Bamboo skewer

Layer two strips

Tip

Press

Table

After rolling the bead, gently press both ends against the table to align the layers of paper.

3. Apply a coating agent to the beads, making sure to cover the tops and bottoms of the beads.

How to Make the Necklace

1. String the paper beads onto the chain.

2. Use the jump rings to attach the lobster clasp and extender chain (refer to page 47 for instructions on attaching jump rings).

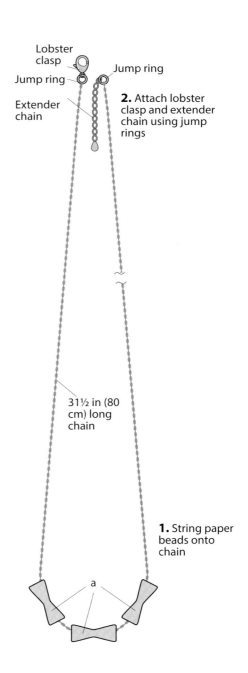

Lobster clasp

Jump ring

Jump ring

Extender chain

2. Attach lobster clasp and extender chain using jump rings

31½ in (80 cm) long chain

1. String paper beads onto chain

a

How to Make the Paper Beads for the Bracelets

1. Cut the paper strips as noted in the diagrams below (also refer to the Paper Bead Chart on page 104). Note that millimeters are the measurement units used in the diagram. If you'd prefer to work in inches, conversions are provided below.

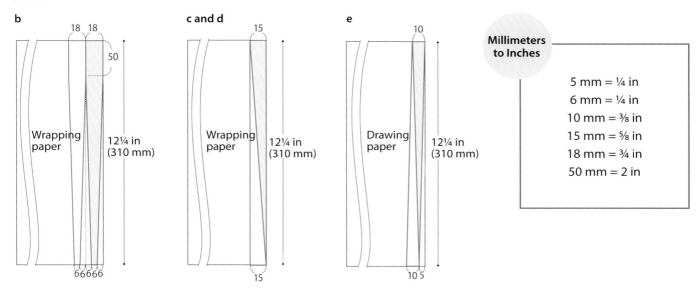

b

18 18

50

Wrapping paper

12¼ in (310 mm)

66666

c and d

15

Wrapping paper

12¼ in (310 mm)

15

e

10

Drawing paper

12¼ in (310 mm)

10 5

Millimeters to Inches

5 mm = ¼ in
6 mm = ¼ in
10 mm = ⅜ in
15 mm = ⅝ in
18 mm = ¾ in
50 mm = 2 in

2. Roll the beads using a chopstick, then secure with a dab of glue. Refer to steps 3 and 4 on page 46 for tips on rolling beads with two strips.

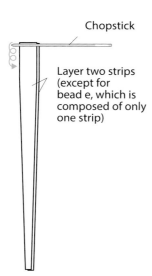

Chopstick

Layer two strips (except for bead e, which is composed of only one strip)

3. Apply a coating agent to the beads.

4. Glue a grommet to each end of each bead. Refer to steps 6 and 7 on pages 52 and 53 for tips on attaching grommets to beads.

b

4 mm grommets

c and d

4 mm grommet

5 mm grommet

e

4mm grommets

How to Make the Bracelets

1. For each bracelet, string the paper beads onto the stretch ribbon (refer to diagrams for layout). For Bracelet B only, string three twisted jump rings onto each side of the bead.

2. Tie the ribbon into a loop using a single knot (see page 60).

Bracelet A

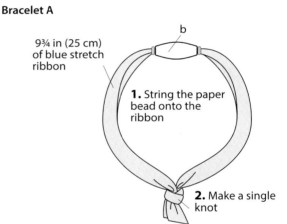

b

9¾ in (25 cm) of blue stretch ribbon

1. String the paper bead onto the ribbon

2. Make a single knot

Bracelet B

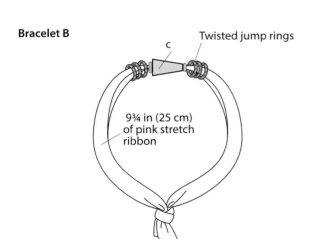

c

Twisted jump rings

9¾ in (25 cm) of pink stretch ribbon

Bracelet C

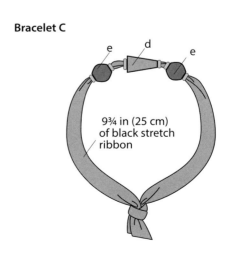

e   d   e

9¾ in (25 cm) of black stretch ribbon

Silk Ribbon Bracelet

Shown on page 32

Finished Size:
11¾ in (30 cm)

Materials

For the paper beads
- One 8½ x 11 in (22 x 28 cm) sheet of yellow drawing paper
- Two small candy wrappers, about 2¼ x 2¾ in (6 x 7 cm) each

For the bracelet
- One 14 mm antique gold charm
- One 6 mm antique gold open jump ring

- 15¾ in (40 cm) of 1 in (2.5 cm) wide yellow silk ribbon

Tools
- Glue
- Bamboo skewer
- Coating agent
- Flat nose pliers
- Beading needle

Paper Bead Chart

Bead	Base Paper	Outside Paper	Strips to Cut	Number of Beads	Finished Size	Rolling Tool
a	Drawing paper	Candy wrapper	2 rectangles	2	About 1 in (25 mm)	Bamboo skewer
b			1 rectangle each	1	About ¾ in (20 mm)	
c				1	About ⅝ in (15 mm)	
d			3 rectangles	3	About ⅜ in (10 mm)	

How to Make the Paper Beads

1. Glue the candy wrappers to the lower right corner of the drawing paper. Cut the paper strips as noted in the diagram (also refer to the Paper Bead Chart above). Note that millimeters are the measurement units used in the diagram. If you'd prefer to work in inches, conversions are provided at right.

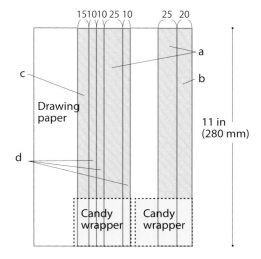

Millimeters to Inches

10 mm = ⅜ in
15 mm = ⅝ in
20 mm = ¾ in
25 mm = 1 in

2. Roll the beads using a bamboo skewer, then secure with a dab of glue (refer to page 42 for basic technique). Note: The candy wrappers should be visible on the outsides of the beads.

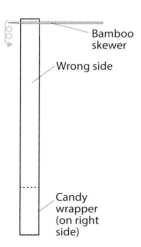

Bamboo skewer

Wrong side

Candy wrapper (on right side)

3. Apply a coating agent to the beads.

How to Make the Bracelet

1. Thread the beading needle with the ribbon.

2. Make a single knot (see page 60). String the paper beads onto the ribbon, making a single knot between each bead (refer to the diagram at right for bead layout). Make a single knot after the final bead.

3. Attach the charm to the jump ring, then string the jump ring onto the ribbon (refer to page 47 for instructions on attaching jump rings).

4. Tie a knot to secure the bracelet around your wrist.

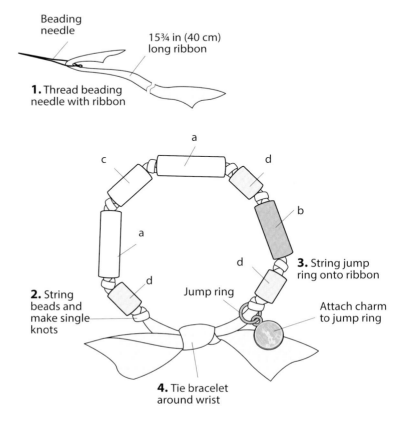

Beading needle

15¾ in (40 cm) long ribbon

1. Thread beading needle with ribbon

2. String beads and make single knots

3. String jump ring onto ribbon

Attach charm to jump ring

Jump ring

4. Tie bracelet around wrist

a c d b a d

Postage Stamp Bracelets

Shown on page 33

Finished Size:
9¾ in (25 cm)

Materials (for one bracelet)

For the paper bead
- One 8½ x 11 in (22 x 28 cm) sheet of copy paper
- One postage stamp

For the bracelet
- Two 5 mm gold grommets
- Two 3 x 10 mm gold rondelle spacer beads
- 11¾ in (30 cm) of ½ in (12 mm) wide stretch velvet ribbon in pink, brown, or blue

Tools
- Glue
- Chopstick (5 mm diameter)
- Coating agent

Paper Bead Chart

Base Paper	Outside Paper	Strips to Cut	Number of Beads	Finished Size	Rolling Tool
Copy paper	Postage stamp	1 rectangle	1	About ⅝–1 in (15-25 mm)	Chopstick

How to Make the Paper Bead

1. Adhere the postage stamp to the lower right corner of the copy paper. Cut the paper strip as noted in the diagram below (also refer to the Paper Bead Chart above). Note: The strip width will vary based on the width of your stamp.

2. Roll the bead using a chopstick, then secure with a dab of glue (refer to page 42 for basic technique). Note: The postage stamp should be visible on the outside of the bead.

Width of stamp (usually ⅝-1 in [15- 25 mm])

Copy paper

11 in (280 mm)

Adhere postage stamp

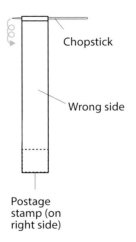

Chopstick

Wrong side

Postage stamp (on right side)

3. Apply a coating agent to the bead.

4. Glue a grommet to each end of the bead. Refer to steps 6 and 7 on pages 52 and 53 for tips on attaching grommets to beads.

Grommets

How to Make the Bracelet

1. String the beads onto the ribbon (refer to the diagram for bead layout).

2. Tie the ribbon into a loop using a single knot (see page 60).

3. Trim the ends at an angle.

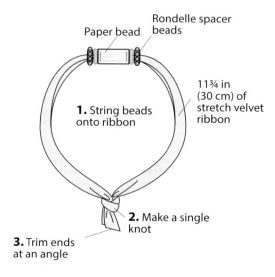

Paper bead

Rondelle spacer beads

1. String beads onto ribbon

11¾ in (30 cm) of stretch velvet ribbon

2. Make a single knot

3. Trim ends at an angle

Long Pendant Necklace & Brooch

Shown on page 33

Finished Size:
Necklace: 33½ in (85 cm)
Brooch: 2 in (5 cm)

Materials

Necklace
For the paper bead
- One 8½ x 11 in (22 x 28 cm) sheet from a theater program or travel brochure
- Two 2.5 mm gold grommets

For the necklace
- One 7 x 15 mm clear and red Czech glass oval bead
- One 6 mm red Czech fire-polished glass bead
- One 10 mm antique gold open jump ring
- Three 4.5 mm antique gold open jump rings
- Three 1¼ in (30 mm) antique gold ball tip headpins
- One 33½ in (85 cm) long antique gold chain

Brooch
For the paper beads
- One 8½ x 11 in (22 x 28 cm) sheet from a theater program or travel brochure

For the brooch
- One 7 mm clear and red Czech glass oval bead
- One 6 mm red Czech fire-polished glass bead
- One 6 x 7 mm antique gold faceted rondelle bead
- One 12 x 23 mm antique gold owl charm
- Three 6 mm antique gold open jump rings
- One 50 mm antique gold kilt pin
- Two 1¼ in (30 mm) antique gold ball tip headpins

Tools
- Glue
- Bamboo skewer
- Coating agent
- Round nose pliers
- Flat nose pliers
- Nipper pliers

Paper Bead Chart

	Bead	Paper Type	Strips to Cut	Number of Beads	Finished Size	Rolling Tool
Necklace	a	Theater program	1 trapezoid	1	About ¾ in (20 mm)	Bamboo skewer
Brooch	b	Theater program	2 trapezoids	1	About ⅜ in (10 mm)	Bamboo skewer
	c		1 trapezoid	1	About ⅜ in (10 mm)	
	d		1 rectangle	1	About ⅜ in (10 mm)	

How to Make the Paper Bead for the Necklace

1. Cut the paper strip as noted in the diagram below (also refer to the Paper Bead Chart on page 112). Note that millimeters are the measurement units used in the diagram. If you'd prefer to work in inches, conversions are provided below.

a

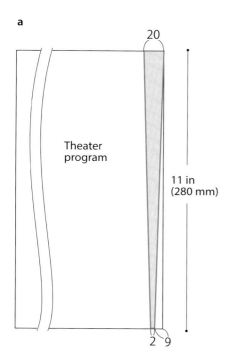

Theater program

20

11 in
(280 mm)

2   9

Millimeters to Inches

2 mm = ¹⁄₁₆ in
9 mm = ⅜ in
20 mm = ¾ in

2. Roll the bead using a bamboo skewer, then secure with a dab of glue (refer to page 42 for basic technique).

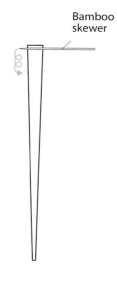

Bamboo skewer

3. Apply a coating agent to the bead.

4. Glue a grommet to each end of the bead. Refer to steps 6 and 7 on pages 52 and 53 for tips on attaching grommets to beads.

Grommets

How to Make the Necklace

1. To make pin parts A-C, string the beads onto the headpins, then make a loop as shown on page 85 (refer to the diagrams for bead layout).

2. Attach pin parts A-C to the 10 mm jump ring. Next, use three 4.5 mm jump rings to attach the 10 mm jump ring to the chain (refer to page 47 for instructions on attaching jump rings).

1. Make pin parts A-C

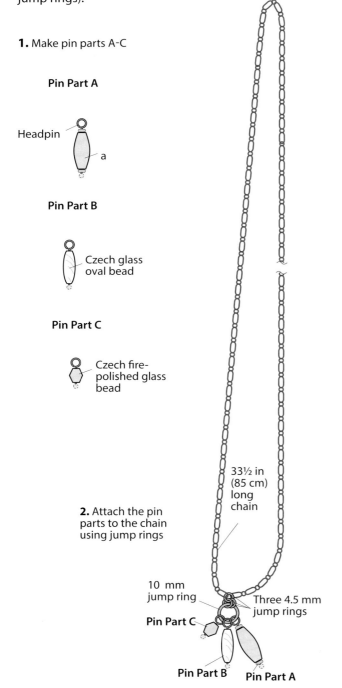

Pin Part A

Headpin

a

Pin Part B

Czech glass oval bead

Pin Part C

Czech fire-polished glass bead

2. Attach the pin parts to the chain using jump rings

33½ in (85 cm) long chain

10 mm jump ring

Three 4.5 mm jump rings

Pin Part C

Pin Part B   **Pin Part A**

How to Make the Brooch

1. To make pin parts A and B, string the beads onto the headpins, then make a loop as shown on page 85.

2. String the paper beads and the rondelle bead onto the kilt pin (refer to the diagram for bead layout).

3. Use jump rings to attach the pin parts and the owl charm to the kilt pin (refer to page 47 for instructions on attaching jump rings).

1. Make pin parts A and B

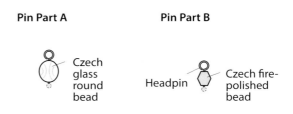

Pin Part A

Czech glass round bead

Pin Part B

Headpin

Czech fire-polished bead

2. String the beads onto the kilt pin

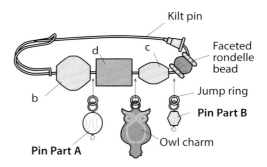

Kilt pin

d   c

Faceted rondelle bead

Jump ring

Pin Part B

b

Owl charm

Pin Part A

3. Use jump rings to attach the pin parts and owl charm

See page 115 for instructions on making the paper beads for the brooch.

How to Make the Paper Beads for the Brooch

1. Cut the paper strips as noted in the diagrams below (also refer to the Paper Bead Chart on page 112). Note that millimeters are the measurement units used in the diagrams. If you'd prefer to work in inches, conversions are provided below.

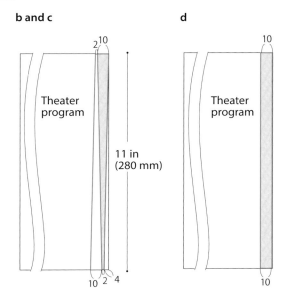

b and c

d

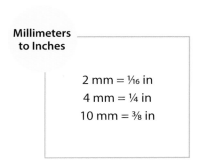

Millimeters to Inches

2 mm = 1/16 in

4 mm = 1/4 in

10 mm = 3/8 in

2. Roll the beads using a bamboo skewer, then secure with a dab of glue. Refer to steps 3 and 4 on page 46 for tips on rolling beads with two strips.

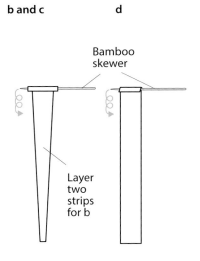

b and c

d

Bamboo skewer

Layer two strips for b

3. Apply a coating agent to the beads.

Liberty & Ribbon Long Necklace

Shown on page 34

Finished Size:
60¾ in (154 cm)

Materials

For the beads
- 67 in (170 cm) of 1½ in (4 cm) wide green Liberty print bias tape (unfolded width)
- 59 in (150 cm) of ⅝ in (1.5 cm) wide blue striped double-fold bias tape
- 67 in (170 cm) of ⅝ in (1.5 cm) wide blue grosgrain ribbon

For the necklace
- 54 6 mm round blue Czech glass beads
- 66 6 mm silver flower-shaped spacer beads

- Two 8 mm silver open jump rings
- Two silver bead tips
- Two small round beads (to be used inside the bead tips)
- 133¾ in (340 cm) of ⅛ in (3 mm) wide blue suede tape
- 94½ in (240 cm) of No. 3 nylon beading cord

Tools
- Fabric glue
- Bamboo skewer
- Coating agent
- Flat nose pliers
- Beading needle

Bead Chart

Bead	Fabric Type	Fabric Color	Strips to Cut	Number of Beads	Finished Size	Rolling Tool
a	Bias tape	Green Liberty print	11 rectangles each	11	About ⅝ in (15 mm)	Bamboo skewer
b		Blue stripe		11		
c	Grosgrain ribbon	Gray		11		

How to Make the Beads

1. Press the bias tapes as noted in the diagrams below, then cut the bias tapes and ribbon into strips (also refer to the Bead Chart above).

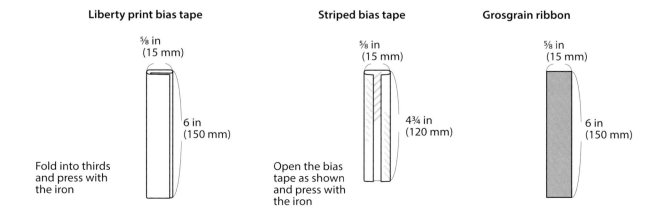

Liberty print bias tape

⅝ in (15 mm)

6 in (150 mm)

Fold into thirds and press with the iron

Striped bias tape

⅝ in (15 mm)

4¾ in (120 mm)

Open the bias tape as shown and press with the iron

Grosgrain ribbon

⅝ in (15 mm)

6 in (150 mm)

2. Roll the beads using a bamboo skewer, then secure with a dab of fabric glue (refer to page 42 for basic technique). Note: You may need to apply a few dabs of glue to hold the bead together as you roll.

Bamboo skewer

3. Apply a coating agent to the beads.

How to Make the Necklace

1. String a bead tip and crimp bead onto the center of the nylon cord. Install the bead tip as shown on page 47.

2. Fold the nylon cord in half. Thread a beading needle with both strands of the nylon cord.

3. String the beads onto both strands (refer to the diagram on page 118 for bead layout).

4. Install the remaining bead tip and crimp bead at the end of the necklace, as shown on page 47.

5. Cut the suede tape into two 67 in (170 cm) long pieces. Fold each piece in half and loop it through a jump ring. Work three-strand braids (refer to page 65) for 11 in (28 cm). Note: The folded half of the tape will count as one strand.

6. Make a single knot (see page 60) at the end of each three-strand braid.

7. Trim the ends, leaving 1½ in (4 cm) of tape after the knot.

8. Use round nose pliers to curl the hook of each bead tip and attach it to a jump ring (refer to step 4 on page 47).

9. Tie the braids together with a single knot to form the necklace into a loop.

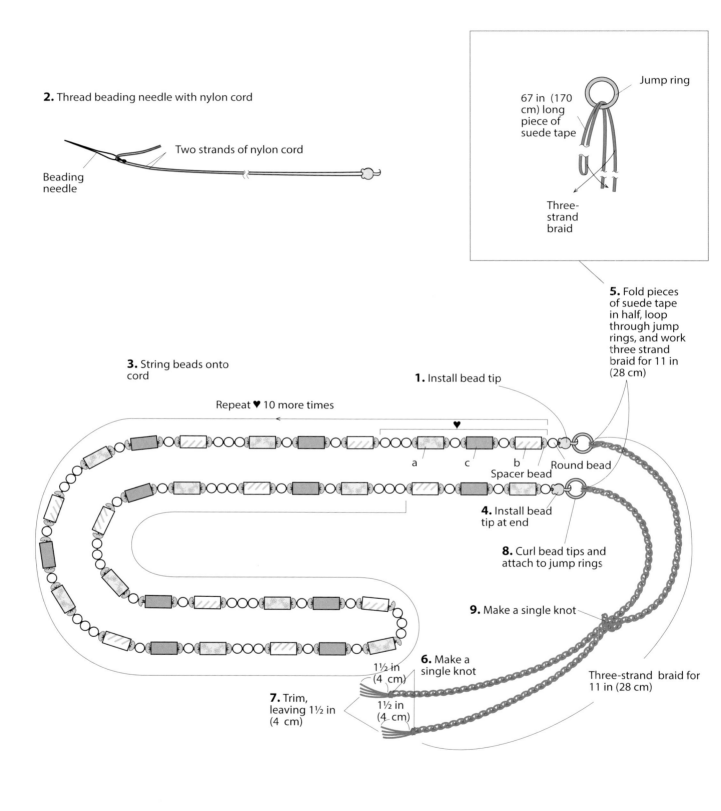

2. Thread beading needle with nylon cord

Two strands of nylon cord

Beading
needle

67 in (170 cm) long piece of suede tape

Jump ring

Three-strand braid

5. Fold pieces of suede tape in half, loop through jump rings, and work three strand braid for 11 in (28 cm)

3. String beads onto cord

1. Install bead tip

Repeat ♥ 10 more times

♥

a   c   b

Round bead

Spacer bead

4. Install bead tip at end

8. Curl bead tips and attach to jump rings

9. Make a single knot

Three-strand braid for 11 in (28 cm)

6. Make a single knot

1½ in (4 cm)

1½ in (4 cm)

7. Trim, leaving 1½ in (4 cm)

Colorful Suede Bracelet

Shown on page 35

Finished Size:
8¾ in (22 cm)

Materials

For the beads
- 1¼ x 3 in (3 x 7.5 cm) pieces of suede in yellow, gray, and blue
- ⅝ x 3 in (1.5 x 7.5 cm) pieces of suede in pink and navy

For the bracelet
- One 3 x 4 mm round brass bead
- 59 in (150 cm) of DMC Pearl Cotton No. 5 embroidery floss in navy (#336)

Tools
- Glue
- Toothpicks
- Beading needle

Bead Chart

Bead	Fabric Type	Color	Strips to Cut	Number of Beads	Finished Size	Rolling Tool
a	Suede	Yellow	2 isosceles triangles	2	About ⅝ in (15 mm)	Toothpick
b		Gray		2		
c		Blue		2		
d		Pink	1 isosceles triangle	1		
e		Navy		1		

How to Make the Beads

1. Cut the suede strips as noted in the diagrams below (also refer to the Paper Bead Chart above). Note that millimeters are the measurement units used in the diagram. If you'd prefer to work in inches, conversions are provided below.

a-c

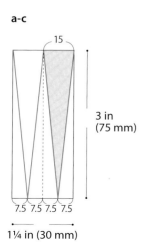

15

3 in (75 mm)

7.5 7.5 7.5 7.5

1¼ in (30 mm)

d and e

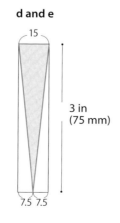

15

3 in (75 mm)

7.5 7.5

Millimeters to Inches

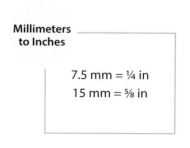

7.5 mm = ¼ in
15 mm = ⅝ in

2. Roll the beads using a toothpick, then secure with a dab of glue (refer to page 42 for basic technique). Note: You may need to apply a few dabs of glue to hold the bead together as you roll.

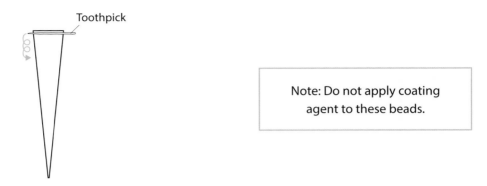

Toothpick

Note: Do not apply coating agent to these beads.

How to Make the Bracelet

1. Cut the embroidery floss into three 19¾ in (50 cm) long pieces. Work a three-strand braid (see page 65) for the entire length of the floss.

2. Use a beading needle to string the beads onto the braid (refer to the diagram for bead layout).

3. Insert both ends of the braid through the round bead.

4. Make a single knot at the end of each braid (see page 60).

5. Trim the braid ends.

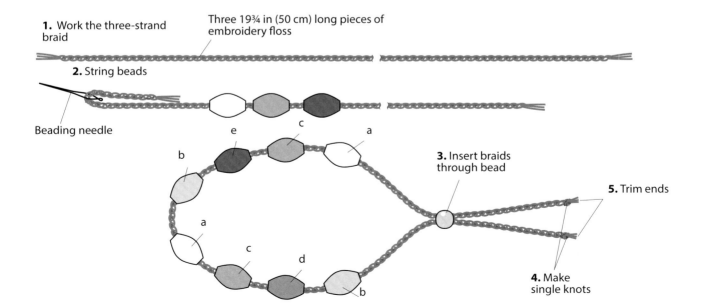

1. Work the three-strand braid

Three 19¾ in (50 cm) long pieces of embroidery floss

2. String beads

Beading needle

e

c

a

b

3. Insert braids through bead

5. Trim ends

a

c

d

b

4. Make single knots

Suede Tassel Pendant

Shown on page 35

Finished Size:
38½ in (98 cm)

Materials

For the bead
- 2¼ x 3 in (5.5 x 7.5 cm) piece of navy suede

For the necklace
- Two 3 x 4 mm round gold beads
- Two 5 mm gold open jump rings
- One 2½ in (65 mm) gold eyepin
- 16 in (40 cm) of DMC Pearl Cotton No. 5 embroidery floss in gold (#5282)
- 51¼ in (130 cm) of DMC Pearl Cotton No. 5 embroidery floss in navy (#336)
- One 35½ in (90 cm) long gold chain

Tools
- Glue
- Bamboo skewer
- Round nose pliers
- Flat nose pliers
- Nipper pliers

Bead Chart

Bead	Fabric Type	Color	Strips to Cut	Number of Beads	Finished Size	Rolling Tool
a	Suede	Navy	1 rectangle	1	About 2¼ in (55 mm)	Bamboo skewer

Wrapped Knot

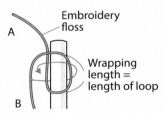

1. Make a loop with the embroidery floss and align on top of the bead or tassel as shown above. Wrap B around the loop without leaving any gaps.

2. Once the wraps are the desired length, insert B through the bottom loop.

3. Pull A to tighten the knot and hide the bottom loop under the wraps. Trim A and B close to the wraps.

How to Make the Bead

1. Cut the suede strip as noted in the diagram below (also refer to the Bead Chart on page 121). Roll the bead using a bamboo skewer, then secure with a dab of glue (refer to page 42 for basic technique). Note: Do not apply coating agent to the bead.

a

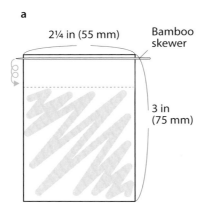

2¼ in (55 mm)

Bamboo skewer

3 in (75 mm)

2. Cut the gold embroidery floss into two 8 in (20 cm) long pieces. Use each piece to make a ⅛ in (3 mm) wide wrapped knot about ¼ in (5 mm) from the end of the bead (see page 121).

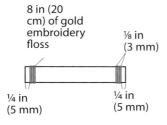

8 in (20 cm) of gold embroidery floss

⅛ in (3 mm)

¼ in (5 mm)

¼ in (5 mm)

3. String a round bead, the suede bead, then another round bead onto the eyepin. Curl the end of the eyepin into a loop as shown on page 85.

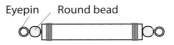

Eyepin   Round bead

4. Bend into a U shape.

How to Make the Necklace

1. Attach the chain to each end of the eyepin using the process used to attach jump rings (refer to page 47).

2. Make the tassel as shown in the diagram below.

3. Use a jump ring to attach the tassel to one end of the eyepin.

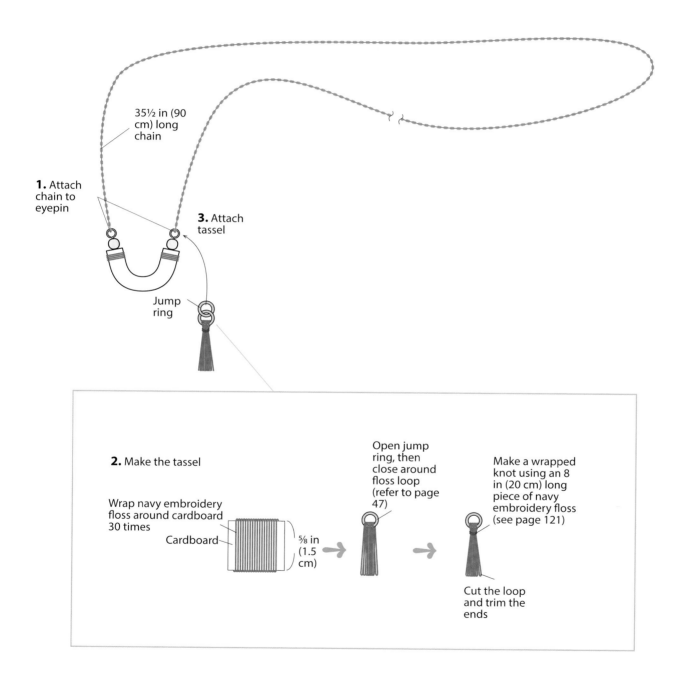

35½ in (90 cm) long chain

1. Attach chain to eyepin

3. Attach tassel

Jump ring

2. Make the tassel

Wrap navy embroidery floss around cardboard 30 times

Cardboard

⅝ in (1.5 cm)

Open jump ring, then close around floss loop (refer to page 47)

Make a wrapped knot using an 8 in (20 cm) long piece of navy embroidery floss (see page 121)

Cut the loop and trim the ends

The Earring Collection

Shown on page 36

Finished Sizes:
Elegant Dangles: 2¼ in
(5.5 cm)
Tropical Hoops: 1 x 2¼ in
(2.5 x 5.5 cm)
Fiesta Dangles: 1½ in (4 cm)
Ocean Drops: 1 in (2.5 cm)
Pearl Hoops: 1½ in (4 cm)
Moon Drops: 1½ in (4 cm)
Modern Hoops: 1¼ x 1½ in
(3 x 3.5 cm)

Materials

Elegant Dangles
For the paper beads
- One 8½ x 11 in (22 x 28 cm) sheet of copy paper printed with a green and light blue pattern
- Eight 2.5 mm gold grommets

For the earrings
- Two 11 mm gold twisted open jump rings
- Two 1¼ in (30 mm) gold eyepins
- Two 1¼ in (30 mm) gold ball tip headpins
- Two gold hook earwires

Tropical Hoops
For the paper beads
- One 8½ x 11 in (22 x 28 cm) sheet of green floral print wrapping paper
- One 8½ x 11 in (22 x 28 cm) sheet each of drawing paper in lime green, green, and turquoise

For the earrings
- Two 6 mm round gold textured beads
- Two 4 mm round gold textured beads
- Two 25 x 40 mm gold teardrop hoop earwires
- Two gold hook earwires

Fiesta Dangles
For the paper beads
- One 8½ x 11 in (22 x 28 cm) sheet each of drawing paper in purple and black
- One 8½ x 11 in (22 x 28 cm) sheet of white copy paper printed with ¼ in (4 mm) wide purple stripes
- 12 2.5 mm gold grommets

For the earrings
- Ten 4.5 mm gold open jump rings
- Six ¾ in (20 mm) gold headpins
- Two gold hook earwires

Ocean Drops
For the paper beads
- One 8½ x 11 in (22 x 28 cm) sheet of blue drawing paper
- Two 2.5 mm gold grommets

For the earrings
- Two 8 mm gold flower spacer beads
- Two 1¼ in (20 mm) gold ball tip headpins
- Two gold hook earwires

Pearl Hoops
For the paper beads
- One sheet of newspaper
- Acrylic paint in pearl white
- Four 2.5 mm gold grommets

For the earrings
- Two 1¼ in (30 mm) gold ball tip headpins
- Two gold oval hoop earrings

Moon Drops

For the paper beads
- One 8½ x 11 in (22 x 28 cm) sheet of white drawing paper
- Four 2.5 mm gold grommets

For the earrings
- 20 4 mm champagne pearls
- Two 1¼ in (30 mm) gold eyepins
- 14 1 in (25 mm) gold headpins
- Two gold hook earwires

Modern Hoops

For the paper beads
- One 8½ x 11 in (22 x 28 cm) sheet of white copy paper printed with ¹⁄₁₆ in (2 mm) wide black zigzags
- Four 2.5 mm gold grommets

For the earrings
- Four 4 mm round black Czech glass beads
- Four 2 mm round black Czech glass beads
- 26 gauge Artistic Wire in non-tarnish brass
- Two gold round hoop earrings

Tools
- Glue
- Bamboo skewer
- Toothpicks
- Coating agent
- Round nose pliers
- Flat nose pliers
- Nipper pliers

Paper Bead Chart

Earrings	Bead	Paper Type	Paper Color	Strips to Cut	Number of Beads	Finished Size	Rolling Tool
Elegant Dangles	a	Copy paper	Green and light blue pattern	4 right triangles	4	About ⅝ in (15 mm)	Toothpick
Tropical Hoops	b	Wrapping paper	Green floral print	2 isosceles triangles each	2	About ¼ x ⅜ in (4 x 9 mm)	Bamboo skewer
	c	Drawing paper	Lime green		2		
	d		Green		2		
	e		Turquoise		2		
Fiesta Dangles	f	Drawing paper	Purple	2 right triangles each	2	About ½ in (13 mm)	Bamboo skewer
	g		Black		2		
	h	Copy paper	¼ in (4 mm) purple stripes		2		
Ocean Drops	i	Drawing paper	Blue	2 isosceles triangles	2	About ⅜ in (10 mm)	Toothpick
Pearl Hoops	j	Newspaper	Painted with pearl white	4 isosceles triangles	2	About ¼ in (7 mm)	Toothpick
Moon Drops	k	Drawing paper	White	4 isosceles triangles	2	About ½ in (12 mm)	Bamboo skewer
Modern Hoops	l	Copy paper	⅛ in (2 mm) wide black zigzags	2 rectangles	2	About ½ in (13 mm)	Toothpick

How to Make the Paper Beads

1. For each variation, cut the paper strips as noted in the diagrams below (also refer to the Paper Bead Chart on page 125). Roll the beads using a bamboo skewer or toothpick, then secure with a dab of glue (refer to page 42 for basic technique). For the Pearl Hoops and Moon Drops, refer to steps 3 and 4 on page 46 for tips on rolling beads with two strips. Apply a coating agent to the beads (refer to page 42). For all variations except the Tropical Hoops, install the grommets as shown on page 53. Note that millimeters are the measurement units used in the diagrams. If you'd prefer to work in inches, conversions are provided below.

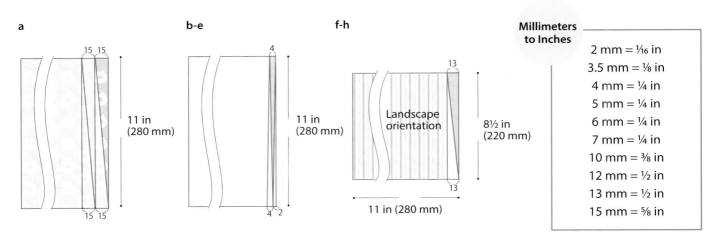

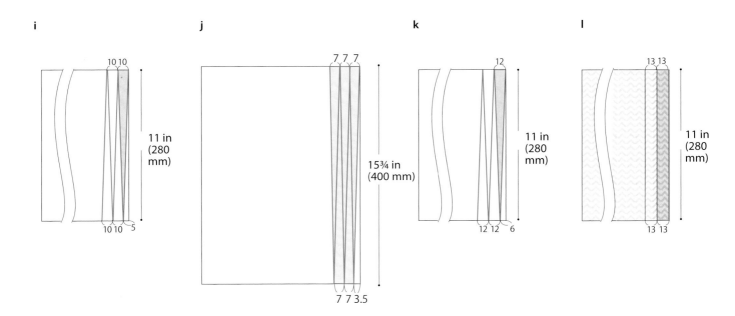

How to Make the Earrings (make 2 of each)

Elegant Dangles

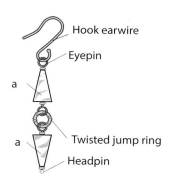

1. String a paper bead onto each eyepin and headpin. Curl the tips of the pins into loops as shown on page 85.

2. Attach an eyepin and headpin loop to each twisted jump ring (refer to page 47 for instructions on attaching jump rings). Next, attach the eyepin loop to the hook earwire.

Tropical Hoops

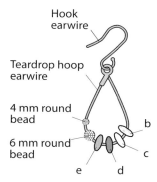

1. String the beads onto the teardrop hoop earwire following the layout shown in the diagram above.

2. Close the hoop and attach it to the hook earwire.

Fiesta Dangles

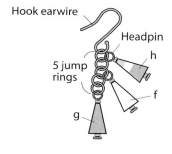

1. String the paper beads onto the headpins, then curl the tips of the pins into loops as shown on page 85.

2. Connect five jump rings (refer to page 47 for instructions on attaching jump rings). Attach the pin parts to the jump rings, then attach the top jump ring to the hook earwire.

Ocean Drops

1. String the paper bead and the flower spacer bead onto the headpin, then curl the tip of the pin into a loop as shown on page 85.

2. Attach the loop to the hook earwire.

Pearl Hoops

Moon Drops

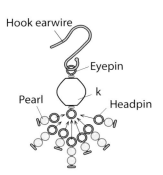

1. String the paper bead onto the headpin, then curl the tip of the pin into a loop as shown on page 85.

2. Attach the loop to the hoop earring.

1. String the paper bead onto the eyepin, then curl the tip of the pin into a loop as shown on page 85.

2. String the pearls onto the headpins as shown in the diagram above, then curl the tips of the pins into loops.

3. Connect the headpin loops to the loop of the eyepin with the paper bead.

4. Attach the other loop of the eyepin to the hook earwire.

Modern Hoops

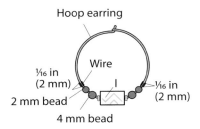

1. String the beads onto the hoop earring, following the layout shown in the diagram above.

2. Wrap wire around the hoop earring on each side of the beads for ¹⁄₁₆ in (2 mm) in order to hold the beads in place.